"The greatest piece of anti-war literature there is in the world was written 2,350 years ago. This is a statement worth a thought or two. Nothing since, no description or denunciation of war's terrors and futilities, ranks with **THE TROJAN WOMEN**, which was put upon the Athenian stage by Euripides in the year 416 B.C. In that faraway age a man saw with perfect clarity what war was, and wrote what he saw in a play of surpassing power, and then—nothing happened."

—Edith Hamilton, translator of **THE TROJAN WOMEN** by Euripides.

CINERAMA RELEASING
Presents
A JOSEF SHAFTEL PRODUCTION

Starring

KATHARINE HEPBURN
VANESSA REDGRAVE
GENEVIEVE BUJOLD
IRENE PAPAS

in a
MICHAEL CACOYANNIS FILM

THE TROJAN WOMEN

with
PATRICK MAGEE
BRIAN BLESSED

Based upon the
Edith Hamilton translation
of the play by Euripides

Screenplay by
MICHAEL CACOYANNIS

Music composed and conducted by
MIKIS THEODORAKIS

Executive Producer
JOSEF SHAFTEL

Produced by
MICHAEL CACOYANNIS
and
ANIS NOHRA

Directed by
MICHAEL CACOYANNIS

In color from
CINERAMA RELEASING

THE TROJAN WOMEN
Euripides

The Play
translated by Edith Hamilton

The Screenplay
by Michael Cacoyannis

Plus
Edith Hamilton's article
"A Pacifist in Periclean Athens"

A Special Introduction by Michael Cacoyannis

A NATIONAL GENERAL COMPANY

THE TROJAN WOMEN
A Bantam Book / published October 1971
2nd printing
3rd printing

Published simultaneously in the United States and Canada

*Bantam Books are published by Bantam Books, Inc., a National
General company. Its trade-mark, consisting of the words "Bantam
Books" and the portrayal of a bantam, is registered in the United
States Patent Office and in other countries. Marca Registrada.
Bantam Books, Inc., 666 Fifth Avenue, New York, N.Y. 10019.*

PRINTED IN THE UNITED STATES OF AMERICA

CONTENTS

A Pacifist in Periclean Athens   1
  by Edith Hamilton

THE TROJAN WOMEN of Euripides   10
  translated by Edith Hamilton

Director's Note   59
  by Michael Cacoyannis

Screenplay for THE TROJAN WOMEN   62
  by Michael Cacoyannis

The Trojan Women

A PACIFIST IN PERICLEAN ATHENS

THE GREATEST PIECE of anti-war literature there is in the world was written 2,350 years ago. This is a statement worth a thought or two. Nothing since, no description or denunciation of war's terrors and futilities, ranks with *The Trojan Women*, which was put upon the Athenian stage by Euripides in the year 416 B.C. In that faraway age a man saw with perfect clarity what war was, and wrote what he saw in a play of surpassing power, and then—nothing happened. No one was won over to his side—no band of eager disciples took up his idea and went preaching it to a war-ridden world. That superlatively efficient war-machine, Rome, described by one of her own historians as having fought continuously for eight hundred years, went on to greater and greater efficiency, with never a glimmer from Euripides to disturb her complacency. In the long annals of literature no writer is recorded who took over his point of view. A few objectors to war are known to us. They crop out sporadically through the ages, but rarely and never with Euripides' deliberate intention of showing war up for what it is. And except for Christ, to whom non-resistance was fundamental, we do not know of anyone else who disbelieved in violence as a means of doing good. None of Christ's followers seem to have followed Him there until comparatively modern times. Not one medieval saint stands out to oppose the thousands of saintly believers in the holiness of this war or that. One soldier there was in the early days of Christianity, a simple, uneducated man,

1

who refused to fight when he was converted, because, as
he explained, Christ did not approve of men killing each
other. But he was easily silenced—and the Church never
denounced his executioners. He never came near to being
made a saint. His very name, Marcellus, is known only
to the curious. That was doctrine too dangerous for the
Fathers of the Church. Christians refuse to fight? Rather,
set up a cross as the banner of a triumphant army, conquering under that standard, killing in His name.

The men of religion, along with the men of letters,
passed by, unseeing, the road Euripides had opened, and
each usually vied with the other in glorifying and mag-
nifying noble, heroic and holy war.

Consider the greatest of all, Shakespeare. He never
bothered to think war through. Of course, that was not
his way with anything. He had another method. Did he
believe in "Contumelious, beastly, mad-brain'd war"?
Or in "Pride, pomp and circumstance of glorious war"?
He says as much on the one side as on the other.

"We few, we happy few, we band of brothers," King
Henry cries before Agincourt:

> This day is called the feast of Crispian;
> And gentlemen of England now abed
> Shall think themselves accursed they were not here,
> And hold their manhoods cheap whiles any speaks
> That fought with us upon Saint Crispin's day.

And then a few pages on:

> If impious war
> Array'd in flames like to the Prince of fiends,
> Do, with his smirched complexion, all fell feats
> Enlink'd to waste and desolation—

It is not possible to know what Shakespeare really
thought about war, if he really thought about it at all.
Always that disconcerting power of imagination blocks
the way to our knowledge of him. He saw eye to eye with
Henry on one page and with the citizens of Harfleur on
the next, and what he saw when he looked only for himself, he did not care to record.

In our Western world Euripides stands alone. He

understood what the world has only begun today to understand.

"The burden of the valley of vision," wrote Isaiah, when he alone knew what could save his world from ruin. To perceive an overwhelmingly important truth of which no one else sees a glimmer, is loneliness such as few even in the long history of the world can have had to suffer. But Euripides suffered it for the greater part of his long life. The valley of vision was his abiding place.

He was the youngest of the three Greek tragic poets, but only a few years younger than Sophocles, who, indeed, survived him. The difference between the two men was great. Each had the keen discernment and the profound spiritual perception of the supreme artist. Each lived and suffered through the long-drawn-out war, which ended in the crushing defeat of Athens, and together they watched the human deterioration brought about during those years. But what they saw was not the same. Sophocles never dreamed of a world in which such things could not be. To him the way to be enabled to endure what was happening, the only way for a man to put life through no matter what happened, was to face facts unwaveringly and accept them, to perceive clearly and bear steadfastly the burden of the human lot, which is as it is and never will be different. To look at the world thus, with profundity, but in tranquillity of spirit, without bitterness, has been given to few, and to no other writer so completely as to Sophocles.

But Euripides saw clearest of all not what is, but what might be. So rebels are made. Great rebels all know the valley of vision. They see possibilities: this evil and that ended; human life transformed; people good and happy. "And there shall be neither sorrow nor crying, nor any more pain: for the former things are passed away." The clarity with which they see brings them anguish; they have a passion of longing to make their vision a reality. They feel, like a personal experience, the giant agony of the world. Not many among the greatest stand higher than Euripides in this aristocracy of humanity.

Sophocles said, "Nothing is wrong which gods command." Euripides said, "If gods do evil, then they are

not gods." Two different worlds are outlined in those two
ideas. Submission is the rule of the first. Not ours to pass
judgment upon the divine. "There are thoughts too great
for mortal men," was ever Sophocles' idea, or, in the
words of another great Greek writer, "To long for the
impossible is a disease of the soul." Keep then within the
rational limit; "Sail not beyond the pillars of Heracles."
But in the second world, Euripides' world, there can be
no submission, because what reigns there is a passion for
justice and a passion of pity for suffering. People who feel
in that way do not submit to the inevitable, or even really
perceive it. But they perceive intolerably what is wrong
and under that tremendous impetus they are ready to
throw all security aside, to call everything into question,
to tear off the veils that hide ugly things, and often,
certainly in Euripides' case, to give up forever peace of
mind.

Two years before the end of the war Euripides died,
not in Athens, but away up north in savage Thrace,
lonelier in his death even than in his life. The reason he
left his city is not recorded, but it was a compelling one.
Men did not give up their home in Greek and Roman
days unless they must. All we are told is a single sentence
in the ancient *Life of Euripides* that he had to go away
because of "the malicious exultation" aroused against
him in the city. It is not hard to discover why.

Athens was fighting a life-and-death war. She did not
want to think about anything. Soldiers must not think.
If they begin to reason why, it is very bad for the army.
Above all, they must not think about the rights and
wrongs of the war. Athens called that being unpatriotic,
not to say traitorous, just as emphatically as the most
Aryan Nazi today could. And Euripides kept making her
think. He put play after play on the stage which showed
the hideousness of cruelty and the pitifulness of human
weakness and human pain. The Athenians took their
theater very seriously, and they were as keen and as sen-
sitive an audience as has ever been in the world. It was
unheard of in Athens to forbid a play because it was not
in accordance with the ruling policy, but many a politi-

cian must have felt very uneasy as he listened to what
Euripides had to say.

The war lasted twenty-seven years. Thucydides, the
great historian of the time, remarks that "War, teaching
men by violence, fits their characters to their condition,"
and two of his austere black-laid-on-white pictures illus-
trate with startling clarity how quickly the Athenians
went downhill under that teaching.

They had been fighting for three years only when an
important island in the Aegean revolted. Athens sent a
big fleet against her and captured her, and in furious
anger voted to put all the men to death and make slaves
of the women and children. They dispatched a ship to
carry the order to the general in command, and then,
true to the spirit of the city that was still so great, they
realized the shocking thing they had done, and they sent
another boat to try to overtake the first and bring it back,
or, if that was impossible, to get to the island in time to
prevent the massacre. We are told how the rowers rowed
as none ever before, and how they did arrive in time.
And Athens felt that weight of guilt lifted, and rejoiced.

But as the war went on men did not feel guilty when
terrible deeds were done. They grew used to them.
Twelve years later, when the war had lasted fifteen years,
another island offended Athens, not by revolting, only by
trying to keep neutral. It was a tiny island, in itself of no
importance, but by that time Athens was incapable of
weighing pros and cons. She took the island, she killed
all the men and enslaved all the women and children,
and we hear of no one who protested. But a few months
later one man showed what he thought, not only of this
terrible deed but of the whole horrible business of war.
Euripides brought out *The Trojan Women*.

There is no plot in *The Trojan Women* and almost no
action. After a ten-year war a town has been taken by
storm and the men in it killed. Except for two subordi-
nate parts the characters are all women. Their husbands
are dead, their children taken from them, and they are
waiting to be shipped off to slavery. They talk about
what has happened and how they feel, and this talk

makes up the substance of the play. They are very unlike
each other, so that we see the situation from different
points of view. There is the wife of the king, an old
woman, whose husband was cut down before her eyes,
in their home as he clung to the altar; her sons, too, are
dead, and she, a queen, is to be a slave to the conquerors.
There is her daughter, a holy virgin, dedicated to the
service of the god of truth, now to be the concubine of
the victorious commander-in-chief. Her daughter-in-law
too, wife of her dearest and most heroic son, she is to
belong to the son of the man who killed him and misused
him after death, Helen, the beautiful, is there as well,
maneuvering to regain her power over the husband she
betrayed, but, in the play, unsuccessful and led away to
die. And there are a number of other women, not great
or impressive at all except through their sufferings, pitiful creatures weeping for the loss of home, husband,
children, and everything sweet and pleasant gone forever.

That is the whole of it. Not one gleam of light anywhere. Euripides had asked himself what war is like
when one looks straight at it, and this is his answer. He
knew his Homer. It was the Greek Bible. And that theme
of glorious poetry about the dauntless deeds of valiant
men, heroically fighting for the most beautiful woman in
the world, turns in his hands into a little group of broken-
hearted women.

A soldier from the victorious army, who comes to bring
them orders, is surprised and irritated to find himself
moved to pity them; but he shrugs his shoulders and
says, "Well—that's war."

The pomp and pride and glorious circumstance are
all gone. When the play opens it is just before dawn, and
the only light in the darkness comes fitfully from the
burning city. Against that background two gods talk to
each other and at once Euripides makes clear what he
thinks about war as a method of improving life in any
way for anyone.

In the old stories about what happened after Troy fell,
told for hundreds of years before Euripides, curiously the
conquering Greeks did not come off well. They had an

exceedingly bad voyage back, and even those who escaped storm and shipwreck found terrible things waiting for them at home. In those faraway times, long before history began, it would seem that some men had learned what our world hardly yet perceives, that inevitably victors and vanquished must in the end suffer together. It was one of those strange prophetic insights which occasionally disturb the sluggish flow of the human spirit, but seem to accomplish nothing for centuries of time. Euripides, however, had discovered the meaning behind the stories.

He makes his two gods decide that the fall of Troy shall turn out no better for the Greeks than for the Trojans. "Give the Greek ships a bitter home-coming," Athena, once the ally of the Greeks, says fiercely to the god of the sea. He agrees that when they set sail for Greece he will "make the wide Aegean roar until shores and reefs and cliffs will hold dead men, bodies of many dead," and when she leaves him he meditates for a moment on human folly: "The fools, who lay a city waste, so soon to die themselves."

"Mother," the Trojan queen's daughter says, "I will show you,

"This town, now, yes, Mother,
  is happier than the Greeks—
They came here to the banks of the Scamander,
and tens of thousands died. For what?
No man had moved their land-marks
or laid siege to their high-walled towns.
But those whom war took never saw their children.
No wife with gentle hand shrouded them for their grave.
They lie in a strange land. And in their homes
are sorrows too, the very same.
Lonely women who died. Old men who waited
for sons that never came.
This is the glorious victory they won.
But we—we Trojans died to save our people.
Oh, fly from war if you are wise. But if war comes,
to die well is to win the victor's crown."

But many whom war kills cannot win that crown. The women talk little about the heroes, much about the helpless. They think of the children who are

> Crying, crying,
> calling to us with tears,
> Mother, I am all alone—

They see the capture of the city through their eyes; the terrible moment of the Greeks' entry as childish ears heard it:

> A shout rang out in the town,
> a cry of blood through the houses,
> and a frightened child caught his mother's skirt
> and hid himself in her cloak,
> while War came forth from his hiding place.

A child's death is the chief action in this play about war. A little boy, hardly grown beyond babyhood, is taken from his mother by the Greeks to be killed. She holds him in her arms and talks to him. She bids him:

Go die, my best-beloved, my own, my treasure,
in cruel hands.
Weeping, my little one? There, there,
you cannot know. You little thing
curled in my arms, how sweet the fragrance of you—
Kiss me. Never again. Come closer, closer—
Your mother who bore you—put your arms around her neck.
Now kiss me, lips to lips—

When the little dead body is brought back, the mother is gone, hurried away to a Greek ship. Only the grandmother is there to receive it. She holds his hands,

> Dear hands, the same dear shape your father's had,
> how loosely now you fall. And dear proud lips
> forever closed.

She remembers the small boy climbing on to her bed in the morning and telling her what he would do when he was grown up.

Not you, but I, old, homeless, childless,
must lay you in your grave, so young,
so miserably dead.

"The poet of the world's grief," Euripides was called:
in this play about war he sounded the deepest depths of
that grief. How not, he would have said, since no other
suffering approaches that which war inflicts.

THE TROJAN WOMEN
of EURIPIDES

━━━━━━━━━━━━━━━━━━━━━━━━━━━━━━━━━━━━

(*The scene is a space of waste ground except for a few
huts to right and left, where the women selected for the
Greek leaders are housed. Far in the background Troy,
the wall in ruins, is slowly burning, as yet more smoke
    than flame. In front a woman with white hair lies on the
ground. It is just before dawn. A tall dim figure is seen,
back of the woman.*)

POSEIDON

I am the sea god. I have come
up from the salt sea depths of the Aegean,
from where the sea nymphs' footsteps fall,
weaving the lovely measures of the dance.
For since that day I built the towers of stone
around this town of Troy, Apollo with me,
—and straight we raised them, true by line and plummet—
good will for them has never left my heart,
my Trojans and their city.
City? Smoke only—all is gone,
perished beneath Greek spears.
A horse was fashioned, big with arms.
Parnassus was the workman's home,
in Phocia, and his name Epeius.
The skill he had Athena gave him.
He sent it through the walls—it carried death.
The wooden horse, so men will call it always,
which held and hid those spears.

10

A desert now where groves were. Blood drips down
from the gods' shrines. Beside his hearth
Priam lies dead upon the altar steps
of Zeus, the hearth's protector.
While to the Greek ships pass the Trojan treasure,
gold, gold in masses, armor, clothing,
stripped from the dead.
The Greeks who long since brought war to the town,
—ten times the seed was sown before Troy fell—
wait now for a fair wind for home,
the joyful sight of wife and child again.
Myself defeated by the Argive goddess
Hera and by Athena, both in league together—
I too must take my leave of glorious Troy,
forsake my altars. When a town is turned
into a desert, things divine fall sick.
Not one to do them honor.
Scamander's stream is loud with lamentation,
so many captive women weeping.
Their masters drew lots for them. Some will go
to Arcady and some to Thessaly.
Some to the lords of Athens, Theseus' sons.
Huts here hold others spared the lot, but chosen
for the great captains.
With them, like them a captive of the spear,
the Spartan woman, Helen.
But if a man would look on misery,
it is here to see—Hecuba lies there
before the gates. She weeps.
Many tears for many griefs.
And one still hidden from her.
But now upon Achilles' grave her daughter
was killed—Polyxena. So patiently she died.
Gone is her husband, gone her sons, all dead.
One daughter whom the Lord Apollo loved,
yet spared her wild virginity, Cassandra,
Agamemnon, in the dark, will force upon his bed.
No thought for what was holy and was God's.
O city happy once, farewell.
O shining towers, crumbling now

beneath Athena's hand, the child of God,
or you would still stand firm on deep foundations.
 (*As he turns to go the goddess* PALLAS ATHENA *enters.*)

ATHENA

Am I allowed to speak to one who is
my father's nearest kinsman,
a god among gods honored, powerful?
If I put enmity aside, will he?

POSEIDON

He will, most high Athena. We are kin,
old comrades too, and these have magic power.

ATHENA

Thanks for your gentleness. What I would say
touches us both, great king.

POSEIDON

A message from the gods? A word from Zeus?
Some spirit, surely?

ATHENA

No, but for Troy's sake, where we stand, I seek
your power to join my own with it.

POSEIDON

What! Now—at last? Has that long hatred left you?
Pity—when all is ashes—burned to ashes?

ATHENA

The point first, please. Will you make common cause
with me? What I wish done will you wish, too?

POSEIDON

Gladly. But what you wish I first must know.
You come to me for Troy's sake or Greece?

ATHENA

I wish to make my Trojan foes rejoice,
and give the Greeks a bitter home-coming.

POSEIDON

The way you change! Here—there—then back again.
Now hate, now love—no limit ever.

ATHENA

You know how I was outraged and my temple.

POSEIDON

Oh that—when Ajax dragged Cassandra out?

ATHENA

And not one Greek to punish him—not one to blame him.

POSEIDON

Even though your power ruined Troy for them.

ATHENA

Therefore with you I mean to hurt them.

POSEIDON

Ready for all you wish. But—hurt them? How?

ATHENA

Give them affliction for their coming home.

POSEIDON

Held here, you mean? Or out on the salt sea?

ATHENA

Whenever the ships sail.
Zeus shall send rain, unending rain, and sleet,
and darkness blown from heaven.
He will give me—he has promised—his thunderbolt,
to strike the ships with fire. They shall burn.
Your part, to make your sea-roads roar—
wild waves and whirlwinds,
while dead men choke the winding bay.
So Greeks shall learn to reverence my house
and dread all gods.

POSEIDON

These things shall be. No need of many words
to grant a favor. I will stir the sea,
the wide Aegean. Shores and reefs and cliffs
will hold dead men, bodies of many dead.
Off to Olympus with you now, and get
those fiery arrows from the hand of Zeus.
Then when a fair wind sends the Greeks to sea,
watch the ships sail.

(Exit ATHENA.*)*
Oh, fools, the men who lay a city waste,
giving to desolation temples, tombs,
the sanctuaries of the dead—so soon
to die themselves.
   (Exit POSEIDON.*)*
   *(The two gods have been talking before daylight, but
   now the day begins to dawn and the woman lying on
   the ground in front moves. She is* HECUBA, *the aged
   queen of Troy.)*

HECUBA

Up from the ground—O weary head, O breaking neck.
This is no longer Troy. And we are not
the lords of Troy.
Endure. The ways of fate are the ways of the wind.
Drift with the stream—drift with fate.
No use to turn the prow to breast the waves.
Let the boat go as it chances.
Sorrow, my sorrow.
What sorrow is there that is not mine,
grief to weep for.
Country lost and children and husband.
Glory of all my house brought low.
All was nothing—nothing, always.
Keep silent? Speak?
Weep then? Why? For what?
   (She begins to get up.)
Oh, this aching body—this bed—
it is very hard. My back pressed to it—
Oh, my side, my brow, my temples.
Up! Quick, quick. I must move.
Oh, I'll rock myself this way, that way,
to the sound of weeping, the song of tears,
dropping down forever.
The song no feet will dance to ever,
for the wretched, the ruined.

O ships, O prows, swift oars,
out from the fair Greek bays and harbors,
over the dark shining sea,

you found your way to our holy city,
and the fearful music of war was heard,
the war song sung to flute and pipe,
as you cast on the shore your cables,
ropes the Nile dwellers twisted and coiled,
and you swung, oh, my grief, in Troy's waters.

What did you come for? A woman?
A thing of loathing, of shame,
to husband, to brother, to home.
She slew Priam, the king,
father of fifty sons,
she wrecked me upon
the reef of destruction.
Who am I that I wait*
here at a Greek king's door?
A slave that men drive on,
an old gray woman that has no home.
Shaven head brought low in dishonor.
O wives of the bronze-armored men who fought,
and maidens, sorrowing maidens,
plighted to shame,
see—only smoke left where was Troy.
Let us weep for her.
As a mother bird cries to her feathered brood,
so will I cry.
Once another song I sang
when I leaned on Priam's scepter,
and the beat of dancing feet
marked the music's measure.
Up to the gods
the song of Troy rose at my signal.
   (*The door of one of the huts opens and a woman
   steals out, then another, and another.*)

FIRST WOMAN

Your cry, O Hecuba—oh, such a cry—
What does it mean? There in the tent

---

* This is the way Professor Murray translates the line and the
one following. The translation is so simple and beautiful, I cannot
bear to give it up for a poorer one of my own.

we heard you call so piteously,
and through our hearts flashed fear.
In the tent we were weeping, too,
for we are slaves.

HECUBA

Look, child, there where the Greek ships lie—

ANOTHER WOMAN

They are moving. The men hold oars.

ANOTHER

O God, what will they do? Carry me off
over the sea in a ship far from home?

HECUBA

You ask and I know nothing,
but I think ruin is here.

ANOTHER WOMAN

Oh, we are wretched. We shall hear the summons.
Women of Troy, go forth from your home,
for the Greeks set sail.

HECUBA

But not Cassandra, oh, not her.
She is mad—she has been driven mad. Leave her within.
Not shamed before the Greeks—not that grief too.
I have enough.
   O Troy, unhappy Troy, you are gone
and we, the unhappy, leave you,
we who are living and we who are dead.
   (*More women now come out from a second hut.*)

A WOMAN

Out of the Greek king's tent
trembling I come, O Queen,
to hear my fate from you.
Not death—They would not think of death
for a poor woman.

ANOTHER

The sailors—they are standing on the prow.
Already they are running out the oars.

ANOTHER

(She comes out of a third hut and several follow her.)
It is so early—but a terror woke me.
  My heart beats so.

ANOTHER

Has a herald come from the Greek camp?
Whose slave shall I be? I—bear that?

HECUBA

Wait for the lot drawing. It is near.

ANOTHER

Argos shall it be, or Phthia?
  or an island of the
  A Greek soldier lead me there,
far, far from Troy?

HECUBA

And I a slave—to whom—where—how?
You old gray woman, patient to endure,
you bee without a sting,
only an image of what was alive.
  Or the ghost of one dead.
I watch a master's door?
  I nurse his children?
  Once I was queen in Troy.

ONE WOMAN TO ANOTHER

Poor thing. What are your tears
to the shame before you?

THE OTHER

The shuttle will still pass through my hands,
  but the loom will not be in Troy.

ANOTHER

  My dead sons. I would look at them once more.
Never again.

ANOTHER

  Worse to come.
A Greek's bed—and I—

ANOTHER

A night like that? Oh, never—
   oh, no—not that for me.

ANOTHER

I see myself a water carrier,
dipping my pitcher in the great Pierian spring.

ANOTHER

   The land of Theseus, Athens, it is known
to be a happy place. I wish I could go there.

ANOTHER

But not to the Eurotas, hateful river,
where Helen lived. Not there, to be a slave
to Menelaus who sacked Troy.

ANOTHER

Oh, look. A man from the Greek army—
a herald. Something strange has happened,
he comes so fast. To tell us—what?
What will he say? Only Greek slaves are here,
waiting for orders.
   (Enter TALTHYBIUS with soldiers.)

TALTHYBIUS

You know me, Hecuba. I have often come
with messages to Troy from the Greek camp.
Talthybius—these many years you've known me.
I bring you news.

HECUBA

It has come, women of Troy. Once we only feared it.

TALTHYBIUS

The lots are drawn, if that is what you feared.

HECUBA

Who—where? Thessaly? Phthia? Thebes?

TALTHYBIUS

A different man takes each. You're not to go together.

HECUBA

Then which takes which? Has any one good fortune?

TALTHYBIUS

I know, but ask about each one, not all at once.

HECUBA

My daughter, who—who drew her? Tell me—
Cassandra. She has had so much to bear.

TALTHYBIUS

King Agamemnon chose her out from all.

HECUBA

Oh! but—of course—to serve his Spartan wife?

TALTHYBIUS

No, no—but for the king's own bed at night.

HECUBA

Oh, never. She is God's, a virgin, always.
That was God's gift to her for all her life.

TALTHYBIUS

He loved her for that same strange purity.*

HECUBA

Throw away, daughter, the keys of the temple.
Take off the wreath and the sacred stole.

TALTHYBIUS

Well, now—a king's bed is not so bad.

HECUBA

My other child you took from me just now?

TALTHYBIUS
(speaking with constraint.)
Polyxena, you mean? Or someone else?

HECUBA

Her. Who drew her?

TALTHYBIUS

They told her off to watch Achilles' tomb.

---

* This line, too, is Professor Murray's, and retained here for the
reason given above.

HECUBA

To watch a tomb? My daughter?
That a Greek custom?
What strange ritual is that, my friend?

TALTHYBIUS

(speaking fast and trying to put her off.)
Just think of her as happy—all well with her.

HECUBA

Those words— Why do you speak like that?
She is alive?

TALTHYBIUS

(determined not to tell her.)
What happened was—well, she is free from trouble.

HECUBA

(wearily giving the riddle up.)
Then Hector's wife—my Hector, wise in war—
Where does she go, poor thing—Andromache?

TALTHYBIUS

Achilles' son took her. He chose her out.

HECUBA

And I, old gray head, whose slave am I,
creeping along with my crutch?

TALTHYBIUS

Slave of the king of Ithaca, Odysseus.

HECUBA

Beat, beat my shorn head! Tear, tear my cheek!
His slave—vile lying man. I have come to this—
There is nothing good he does not hurt—a lawless beast.
He twists and turns, this way and that, and back again.
A double tongue, as false in hate as false in love.
Pity me, women of Troy,
I have gone. I am lost—oh, wretched.
An evil fate fell on me,
a lot the hardest of all.

A WOMAN

You know what lies before you, Queen, but I—
What man among the Greeks owns me?

TALTHYBIUS *(to the soldiers.)*

Off with you. Bring Cassandra here. Be quick,
you fellows. We must give her to the chief,
into his very hand. And then these here
to all the other generals. But what's that—
that flash of light inside there?
  (Light shines through the crevices of one of the huts.)
Set fire to the huts—is that their plan,
these Trojan women? Burn themselves to death
rather than sail to Greece. Choosing to die instead.
How savagely these days the yoke bears down
on necks so lately free.
Open there, open the door. *(Aside.)* As well for them
    perhaps,
but for the Greeks—they'd put the blame on me.

HECUBA

No, no, there is nothing burning. It is my daughter,
Cassandra. She is mad.
  *(CASSANDRA enters from the hut dressed like a priestess,
  a wreath in her hair, a torch in her hand. She does not
  seem to see anyone.)*

CASSANDRA

Lift it high—in my hand— light to bring.
  I praise him. I bear a flame.
  With my torch I touch to fire
  this holy place.
  Hymen, O Hymen.
  Blessed the bridegroom,
  blessed am I
to lie with a king in a king's bed in Argos.
  Hymen, O Hymen.
Mother, you weep
tears for my father dead,
mourning for the beloved
    country lost.
I for my bridal here
lift up the fire's flame
to the dawn, to the splendor,
to you, O Hymen.
Queen of night,

give your starlight
to a virgin bed,
as of old you did.
Fly, dancing feet.
Up with the dance.
    Oh, joy, oh, joy!
Dance for my father dead,
    most blest to die.
Oh, holy dance!
Apollo—you?
Lead on then.
There in the laurel grove
I served your altar.
    Dance, Mother, come.
    Keep step with me.
Dear feet with my feet
    tracing the measure
    this way and that.
Sing to the Marriage god,
oh, joyful song.
Sing for the bride, too,
joyously all.
Maidens of Troy,
dressed in your best,
honor my marriage.
Honor too him
whose bed fate drives me to share.

A WOMAN

Hold her fast, Queen, poor frenzied girl.
She might rush straight to the Greek camp.

HECUBA

O fire, fire, when men make marriages
you light the torch, but this flame flashing here
is for grief only. Child, such great hopes once I had.
I never thought that to your bridal bed
Greek spears would drive you.
Give me your torch. You do not hold it straight,
you move so wildly. Your sufferings, my child,
have never taught you wisdom.
You never change. Here! someone take the torch

into the hut. This marriage needs no songs,
but only tears.

CASSANDRA

O Mother, crown my triumph with a wreath.
Be glad, for I am married to a king.
Send me to him, and if I shrink away,
drive me with violence. If Apollo lives,
my marriage shall be bloodier than Helen's.
Agamemnon, the great, the glorious lord of Greece—
I shall kill him, Mother, lay his house as low
as he laid ours, make him pay for all
he made my father suffer, brothers, and—
But no. I must not speak of that—that axe
which on my neck—on others' too—
nor of that murder of a mother.
All, all because he married me and so
pulled his own house down.
But I will show you. This town now, yes, Mother,
is happier than the Greeks. I know that I am mad,
but Mother, dearest, now, for this one time
I do not rave.
One woman they came hunting, and one love,
Helen, and men by tens of thousands died.
Their king, so wise, to get what most he hated
destroyed what most he loved,
his joy at home, his daughter, killing her
for a brother's sake, to get him back a woman
who had fled because she wished—not forced to go.
And when they came to the banks of the Scamander
those thousands died. And why?
No man had moved their landmarks
or laid siege to their high-walled towns.
But those whom war took never saw their children.
No wife with gentle hands shrouded them for their grave.
They lie in a strange land. And in their homes
are sorrows, too, the very same.
Lonely women who died, old men who waited
for sons that never came—no son left to them
to make the offering at their graves.
That was the glorious victory they won.

But we—we Trojans died to save our people,
no glory greater. All those the spear slew,
friends bore them home and wrapped them in their
     shroud
with dutiful hands. The earth of their own land
covered them. The rest, through the long days they fought,
had wife and child at hand, not like the Greeks,
whose joys were far away.
And Hector's pain—your Hector. Mother, hear me.
This is the truth: he died, the best, a hero.
Because the Greeks came, he died thus.
Had they stayed home, we never would have known him.
This truth stands firm: the wise will fly from war.
But if war comes, to die well is to win
the victor's crown.
The only shame is not to die like that.
So, Mother, do not pity Troy,
or me upon my bridal bed.

                    TALTHYBIUS
*(has been held awestruck through all this, but can bear
                  no more.)*
Now if Apollo had not made you mad
I would have paid you for those evil words,
bad omens, and my general sailing soon.
     (Grumbles to himself.)
The great, who seem so wise, have no more sense
than those who rank as nothing.
Our king, the first in Greece, bows down
before this mad girl, loves her, chooses her
out of them all. Well, I am a poor man,
but I'd not go to bed with her.
     (Turns to CASSANDRA.)
Now you—you know your mind is not quite right.
So all you said against Greece and for Troy,
I never heard—the wind blew it away.
Come with me to the ship now.
     (Aside.)
A grand match for our general, she is.
     (To HECUBA, *gently.)*

And you, do follow quietly when Odysseus' men come.
His wife's a good, wise woman, so they say.

CASSANDRA

(seeming to see TALTHYBIUS *for the first time and looking
him over haughtily.)*
A strange sort of slave, surely.
Heralds such men are called,
hated by all, for they are tyrants' tools.
You say my mother goes to serve Odysseus?
     (She turns away and speaks to herself.)
But where then is Apollo's word, made clear
to me, that death will find her here?
And—no, that shame I will not speak of.
Odysseus! wretched—but he does not know.
   Soon all these sorrows, mine and Troy's, will seem
compared to his like golden hours.
Ten years behind him here, ten years before him.
Then only, all alone, will he come home,
and there find untold trouble has come first.
But his cares—why let fly one word at him?
Come, let us hasten to my marriage.
We two shall rest, the bridegroom and the bride,
within the house of death.
O Greek king, with your dreams of grandeur yet to come,
vile as you are, so shall your end be,
in darkness—all light gone.
And me—a cleft in the hills,
washed by winter rains,
his tomb near by.
There—dead—cast out—naked—
and wild beasts seeking food—
It is I there—I myself—Apollo's servant.
O flowers of the God I love, mysterious wreaths,
away. I have forgotten temple festival,
I have forgotten joy.
Off. I tear them from my neck.
Swift winds will carry them
up to you, O God of truth.
My flesh still clean, I give them back to you.

Where is the ship? How do I go on board?
Spread the sail—the wind comes swift.
Those who bring vengeance—three are they,
And one of them goes with you on the sea.
Mother, my Mother, do not weep. Farewell,
dear City. Brothers, in Troy's earth laid, my father,
a little time and I am with you.
You dead, I shall come to you a victor.
Those ruined by my hand who ruined us.
    (*She goes out with* TALTHYBIUS *and the soldiers.*
    HECUBA, *motionless for a moment, falls.*)

A WOMAN

The Queen! See—see—she is falling.
Oh, help! She cannot speak.
Miserable slaves, will you leave her on the ground,
old as she is. Up—lift her up.

HECUBA

Let me be. Kindness not wanted is unkindness.
I cannot stand. Too much is on me.
Anguish here and long since and to come—
O God— Do I call to you? You did not help.
But there is something that cries out for God
when trouble comes.
Oh, I will think of good days gone,
days to make a song of,
crowning my sorrow by remembering.
We were kings and a king I married.
Sons I bore him, many sons.
That means little—but fine, brave lads.
They were the best in all Troy.
No woman, Trojan, Greek, or stranger,
had sons like mine to be proud of.
I saw them fall beneath Greek spears.
My hair I shore at the grave of the dead.
Their father—I did not learn from others
that I must weep for him—these eyes beheld him.
I, my own self, saw him fall murdered
upon the altar, when his town was lost.
My daughters, maidens reared to marry kings,
are torn from me. For the Greeks I reared them.

All gone—no hope that I shall look upon
their faces any more, or they on mine.
And now the end—no more can lie beyond—
an old gray slave woman I go to Greece.
The tasks they know for my age hardest, mine.
The door to shut and open, bowing low
—I who bore Hector—meal to grind; upon
the ground lay this old body down that once
slept in a royal bed; torn rags around me,
torn flesh beneath.
And all this misery and all to come
because a man desired a woman.
Daughter, who knew God's mystery and joy,
what strange chance lost you your virginity?
And you, Polyxena—where are you gone?
No son, no daughter, left to help my need,
and I had many, many—
Why lift me up? What hope is there to hold to?
   This slave that once went delicately in Troy,
take her and cast her on her bed of clay,
rocks for her pillow, there to fall and die,
wasted with tears. Count no one happy,
however fortunate, before he dies.

CHORUS

Sing me, O Muse, a song for Troy,
a strange song sung to tears,
a music for the grave.
O lips, sound forth a melody
   for Troy.

A four-wheeled cart brought the horse to the gates,
brought ruin to me,
   captured, enslaved me.
Gold was the rein and the bridle,
deadly the arms within,
and they clashed loud to heaven as the threshold was
   passed.

High on Troy's rock the people cried,
"Rest at last, trouble ended.
Bring the carven image in.

Bear it to Athena,
fit gift for the child of God."

Who of the young but hurried forth?
Who of the old would stay at home?
With song and rejoicing they brought death in,
treachery and destruction.

All that were in Troy,
hastening to the gate,
drew that smooth-planed horse of wood
carven from a mountain pine,
where the Greeks were hiding,
where was Troy's destruction,
gave it to the goddess,
gift for her, the virgin,
driver of the steeds that never die.

With ropes of twisted flax,
as a ship's dark hull is drawn to land,
they brought it to her temple of stone,
to her floor that soon would run with blood,
  to Pallas Athena.

  On their toil and their joy
the dark of evening fell,
but the lutes of Egypt still rang out
  to the songs of Troy.

And girls with feet light as air
dancing, sang happy songs.
The houses blazed with light
through the dark splendor,
  and sleep was not.

A GIRL

I was among the dancers.
I was singing to the maiden of Zeus,
the goddess of the hills.
A shout rang out in the town,
a cry of blood through the houses,
and a frightened child caught his mother's skirt
and hid himself in her cloak.

Then War came forth from his hiding place—
Athena, the virgin, devised it.
Around the altars they slaughtered us.
Within on their beds lay headless men,
young men cut down in their prime.
This was the triumph-crown of Greece.
We shall bear children for her to rear,
grief and shame to our country.
  (*A chariot approaches, loaded with spoils. In it sits a
  woman and a child.*)

A WOMAN

Look, Hecuba, it is Andromache.
See, in the Greek car yonder.
Her breast heaves with her sobs and yet
the baby sleeps there, dear Astyanax,
    the son of Hector.

ANOTHER

Most sorrowful of women, where do you go?
Beside you the bronze armor that was Hector's,
the spoil of the Greek spear, stripped from the dead.
Will Achilles' son use it to deck his temples?

ANDROMACHE

I go where my Greek masters take me.

HECUBA

Oh, our sorrow—our sorrow.

ANDROMACHE

Why should you weep? This sorrow is mine.

HECUBA

O God—

ANDROMACHE

What has come to me is mine.

HECUBA

My children—

ANDROMACHE

  Once we lived, not now.

HECUBA

Gone—gone—happiness—Troy—

ANDROMACHE

And you bear it.

HECUBA

Sons, noble sons, all lost.

ANDROMACHE

Oh, sorrow is here.

HECUBA

For me—for me.

ANDROMACHE

For the city, in its shroud of smoke.
Come to me, O my husband.

HECUBA

What you cry to lies in the grave.
My son, wretched woman, mine.

ANDROMACHE

Defend me—me, your wife.

HECUBA

My son, my eldest son,
whom I bore to Priam,
whom the Greeks used shamefully,
come to me, lead me to death.

ANDROMACHE

Death—oh, how deep a desire.

HECUBA

Such is our pain—

ANDROMACHE

For a city that has fallen, fallen.

HECUBA

For anguish heaped upon anguish.

ANDROMACHE

For the anger of God against Paris,

your son, who fled from death,
who laid Troy's towers low
   to win an evil love.
Dead men—bodies—blood—
vultures hovering—
Oh, Athena the goddess is there, be sure,
and the slave's yoke is laid upon Troy.

HECUBA

O country, desolate, empty.

ANDROMACHE

My tears fall for you.

HECUBA

Look and see the end—

ANDROMACHE

Of the house where I bore my children.

HECUBA

O children, your mother has lost her city,
and you—you have left her alone.
Only grief is mine and mourning.
Tears and more tears, falling, falling.
The dead—they have forgotten their pain.
They weep no more.

A WOMAN *(aside to another.)*

Tears are sweet in bitter grief,
and sorrow's song is lamentation.

ANDROMACHE

Mother of him whose spear of old brought death
to Greeks unnumbered, you see what is here.

HECUBA

I see God's hand that casts the mighty down
and sets on high the lowly.

ANDROMACHE

Driven like cattle captured in a raid,
my child and I—the free changed to a slave.
Oh, changed indeed.

HECUBA

It is fearful to be helpless. Men just now
have taken Cassandra—forced her from me.

ANDROMACHE

And still more for you—more than that—

HECUBA

Number my sorrows, will you? Measure them?
One comes—the next one rivals it.

ANDROMACHE

Polyxena lies dead upon Achilles' tomb,
a gift to a corpse, to a lifeless thing.

HECUBA

My sorrow! That is what Talthybius meant—
I could not read his riddle. Oh, too plain.

ANDROMACHE

I saw her there and left the chariot
and covered her dead body with my cloak,
and beat my breast.

HECUBA

Murdered—my child. Oh, wickedly!
Again I cry to you. Oh, cruelly slain!

ANDROMACHE

She has died her death, and happier by far
dying than I alive.

HECUBA

Life cannot be what death is, child.
Death is empty—life has hope.

ANDROMACHE

Mother, O Mother, hear a truer word.
Now let me bring joy to your heart.
I say to die is only not to be,
and rather death than life with bitter grief.
They have no pain, they do not feel their wrongs.
But the happy who has come to wretchedness,
his soul is a lost wanderer,
the old joys that were once, left far behind.

She is dead, your daughter—to her the same
as if she never had been born.
She does not know the wickedness that killed her.
While I—I aimed my shaft at good repute.
I gained full measure—then missed happiness.
For all that is called virtuous in a woman
I strove for and I won in Hector's house.
Always, because we women, whether right or wrong,
are spoken ill of
unless we stay within our homes, my longing
I set aside and kept the house.
Light talk, glib women's words,
could never gain an entrance there.
My own thoughts were enough for me,
best of all teachers to me in my home.
Silence, a tranquil eye, I brought my husband,
knew well in what I should rule him,
and when give him obedience.
And this report of me came to the Greeks
for my destruction. When they captured me
Achilles' son would have me.
I shall be a slave to those who murdered—
O Hector, my beloved—shall I thrust him aside,
open my heart to the man that comes to me,
and be a traitor to the dead?
And yet to shrink in loathing from him
and make my masters hate me—
One night, men say, one night in a man's bed
will make a woman tame—
Oh, shame! A woman throw her husband off
and in a new bed love another—
Why, a young colt will not run in the yoke
with any but her mate—not a dumb beast
that has no reason, of a lower nature.
O Hector, my beloved, you were all to me,
wise, noble, mighty, in wealth, in manhood, both.
No man had touched me when you took me,
took me from out my father's home
and yoked a girl fast to you.
And you are dead, and I, with other plunder,
am sent by sea to Greece. A slave's yoke there.

Your dead Polyxena you weep for,
what does she know of pain like mine?
The living must have hope. Not I, not any more.
I will not lie to my own heart. No good will ever come.
But oh, to think it would be sweet.

A WOMAN

We stand at the same point of pain. You mourn your ruin,
and in your words I hear my own calamity.

HECUBA

Those ships—I never have set foot on one,
but I have heard of them, seen pictures of them.
I know that when a storm comes which they think
they can ride out, the sailors do their best,
one by the sail, another at the helm,
and others bailing.
But if great ocean's raging overwhelms them,
they yield to fate.
They give themselves up to the racing waves.
So in my many sorrows I am dumb.
I yield, I cannot speak.
The great wave from God has conquered me.
But, O dear child, let Hector be,
and let be what has come to him.
Your tears will never call him back.
Give honor now to him who is your master.
Your sweet ways—use them to allure him.
So doing you will give cheer to your friends.
Perhaps this child, my own child's son,
you may rear to manhood and great aid for Troy,
and if ever you should have more children,
they might build her again. Troy once more be a city!
Oh—one thought leads another on.
But why again that servant of the Greeks?
I see him coming. Some new plan is here.

(Enter TALTHYBIUS *with soldiers. He is troubled and advances hesitatingly.*)

TALTHYBIUS

Wife of the noblest man that was in Troy,

O wife of Hector, do not hate me.
Against my will I come to tell you.
The people and the kings have all resolved—

ANDROMACHE

What is it? Evil follows words like those.

TALTHYBIUS

This child they order— Oh, how can I say it—

ANDROMACHE

Not that he does not go with me to the same master—

TALTHYBIUS

No man in Greece shall ever be his master.

ANDROMACHE

But—leave him here—all that is left of Troy?

TALTHYBIUS

I don't know how to tell you. What is bad,
words can't make better—

ANDROMACHE

I feel you kind. But you have not good news.

TALTHYBIUS

Your child must die. There, now you know
the whole, bad as it is.

ANDROMACHE

Oh, I have heard an evil worse
than a slave in her master's bed.

TALTHYBIUS

It was Odysseus had his way. He spoke
to all the Greeks.

ANDROMACHE

O God. There is no measure to my pain.

TALTHYBIUS

He said a hero's son must not grow up—

ANDROMACHE

God, on his own sons may that counsel fall.

TALTHYBIUS
—but from the towering wall of Troy be thrown.
Now, now—let it be done—that's wiser.
Don't cling so to him. Bear your pain
the way a brave woman suffers.
You have no strength—don't look to any help.
There's no help for you anywhere. Think—think.
The city gone—your husband too. And you
a captive and alone, one woman—how
can you do battle with us? For your own good
I would not have you try, and draw
hatred down on you and be shamed.
Oh, hush—never a curse upon the Greeks.
If you say words that make the army angry
the child will have no burial, and without pity—
Silence now. Bear your fate as best you can.
So then you need not leave him dead without a grave,
and you will find the Greeks more kind.

ANDROMACHE
Go die, my best beloved, my own, my treasure,
in cruel hands, leaving your mother comfortless.
Your father was too noble. That is why
they kill you. He could save others,
he could not save you for his nobleness.
My bed, my bridal—all for misery—
when long ago I came to Hector's halls
to bear my son—oh, not for Greeks to slay,
but for a ruler over teeming Asia.
Weeping, my little one? There, there.
You cannot know what waits for you.
Why hold me with your hands so fast, cling so fast to me?
You little bird, flying to hide beneath my wings.
And Hector will not come—he will not come,
up from the tomb, great spear in hand, to save you.
Not one of all his kin, of all the Trojan might.
How will it be? Falling down—down—oh, horrible.
And his neck—his breath—all broken.
And none to pity. You little thing,
curled in my arms, you dearest to your mother,
how sweet the fragrance of you.

All nothing then—this breast from where
your baby mouth drew milk, my travail too,
my cares, when I grew wasted watching you.
Kiss me— Never again. Come, closer, closer.
Your mother who bore you—put your arms around my
    neck.
Now kiss me, lips to lips.
O Greeks, you have found out ways to torture
that are not Greek.
A little child, all innocent of wrong—
you wish to kill him.
O Helen, evil growth, that was sown by Tyndareus,
you are no child of Zeus, as people say.
Many the fathers you were born of,
Madness, Hatred, Red Death, whatever poison
the earth brings forth—no child of Zeus,
but Greece's curse and all the world's.
God curse you, with those beautiful eyes
that brought to shame and ruin
Troy's far-famed plains.
Quick! take him—seize him—cast him down—
if so you will. Feast on his flesh.
God has destroyed me, and I cannot—
I cannot save my child from death.
Oh hide my head for shame and fling me
into the ship.
    (*She falls, then struggles to her knees.*)
My fair bridal—I am coming—
Oh, I have lost my child, my own.

A WOMAN

O wretched Troy, tens of thousands lost
for a woman's sake, a hateful marriage bed.

TALTHYBIUS
    (*drawing the child away.*)
Come, boy, let go. Unclasp those loving hands,
poor mother.
Come now, up, up, to the very height,
where the towers of your fathers crown the wall,
and where it is decreed that you must die.
    (*To the soldiers.*)

Take him away.
A herald who must bring such orders
should be a man who feels no pity,
and no shame either—not like me.

HECUBA

Child, son of my poor son, whose toil was all in vain,
we are robbed, your mother and I, oh, cruelly—
robbed of your life. How bear it?
What can I do for you, poor piteous child?
Beat my head, my breast—all I can give you.
Troy lost, now you—all lost.
The cup is full. Why wait? For what?
Hasten on—swiftly on to death.

(The soldiers, who have waited while HECUBA *speaks,
go out with the child and* TALTHYBIUS. *One of them
takes* ANDROMACHE *to the chariot and drives off with
her.)*

CHORUS

The waves make a ring around Salamis.
The bees are loud in the island.
King Telamon built him a dwelling.
It fronted the holy hills,
where first the gray gleaming olive
Athena showed to men,
the glory of shining Athens,
her crown from the sky.
He joined himself to the bowman,
the son of Alcmena, for valorous deeds.
Troy, Troy he laid waste, my city,
long ago when he went forth from Greece.
When he led forth from Greece the bravest
in his wrath for the steeds * withheld,
and by fair-flowing Simois stayed his oar
that had brought him over the sea.

---

* When Troy was destroyed the first time, the reason was that
the Trojan king had promised two immortal horses to Hercules
("the son of Alcmena") but did not give them to him. Hercules
in revenge ruined the city. The son of this king was Ganymede,
cup-bearer to Zeus.

Cables there made the ship fast.
In his hand was the bow that never missed.
It brought the king to his death.
Walls of stone that Phoebus had built
he wrecked with the red breath of fire.
He wasted the plain of Troy.
Twice her walls have fallen. Twice
a blood-stained spear struck her down,
    laid her in ruin.

In vain, O you who move
with delicate feet where the wine-cups are gold,
son of that old dead king,
who fill with wine the cup Zeus holds,
service most fair—
she who gave you birth is afire.
The shores of the sea are wailing for her.
As a bird cries over her young,
women weep for husbands, for children,
for the old, too, who gave them birth.
Your dewy baths are gone,
and the race-course where you ran.
Yet your young face keeps the beauty of peace
in joy, by the throne of Zeus.
While Priam's land
lies ruined by Greek spearsmen.

Love, O Love,
once you came to the halls of Troy,
and your song rose up to the dwellers in heaven.
How did you then exalt Troy high,
binding her fast to the gods, by a union—
No—I will not speak blame of Zeus.
But the light of white-winged Dawn, dear to men,
is deadly over the land this day,
shining on fallen towers.
And yet Dawn keeps in her bridal bower
her children's father, a son of Troy.
Her chariot bore him away to the sky.
It was gold, and four stars drew it.
Hope was high then for our town.

But the magic that brought her the love of the gods
has gone from Troy.
(As the song ends MENELAUS *enters with a bodyguard
of soldiers.)*

MENELAUS

How bright the sunlight is today—
this day, when I shall get into my power
Helen, my wife. For I am Menelaus,
the man of many wrongs.
I came to Troy and brought with me my army,
not for that woman's sake, as people say,
but for the man who from my house,
and he a guest there, stole away my wife.
Ah, well, with God's help he has paid the price,
he and his country, fallen beneath Greek spears.
I am come to get her—wretch—I cannot speak her name
who was my wife once.
In a hut here, where they house the captives,
she is numbered with the other Trojan women.
The men who fought and toiled to win her back,
have given her to me—to kill, or else,
if it pleases me, to take her back to Argos.
And it has seemed to me her death in Troy
is not the way. I will take her overseas,
with swift oars speeding on the ship,
and there in Greece give her to those to kill
whose dearest died because of her.
(To his men.)
Attention! Forward to the huts.
Seize her and drag her out by that long blood-drenched
hair—
(Stops suddenly and controls himself.)
And when fair winds come, home with her to Greece.
(Soldiers begin to force the door of one of the huts.)

HECUBA
(comes slowly forward.)
O thou who dost uphold the world,
whose throne is high above the world,
thou, past our seeking hard to find, who art thou?
God, or Necessity of what must be,

or Reason of our reason?
Whate'er thou art, I pray to thee,
seeing the silent road by which
all mortal things are led by thee to justice.

MENELAUS

What have we here? A queer prayer that.

HECUBA

(She comes still nearer to him and he recognizes her.)
Kill her, Menelaus? You will? Oh, blessings on you!
But—shun her, do not look at her.
Desire for her will seize you, conquer you.
For through men's eyes she gets them in her power.
She ruins them and ruins cities too.
Fire comes from her to burn homes,
magic for death. I know her—so do you,
and all these who have suffered.
*(HELEN enters from the hut. The soldiers do not touch
her. She is very gentle and undisturbed.)*

HELEN

(with sweet, injured dignity. Not angry at all.)
Menelaus, these things might well make a woman fear.
Your men with violence have driven me from my room,
have laid their hands upon me.
Of course I know—almost I know—you hate me,
but yet I ask you, what is your decision,
yours and the Greeks? Am I to live or not?

MENELAUS

Nothing more clear. Unanimous, in fact.
Not one who did not vote you should be given me,
whom you have wronged, to kill you.

HELEN

Am I allowed to speak against the charge?
To show you if I die that I shall die
most wronged and innocent?

MENELAUS

I have come to kill you, not to argue with you.

HECUBA

Oh, hear her. She must never die unheard.

Then, Menelaus, let me answer her.
The evil that she did in Troy, you do not know.
But I will tell the story. She will die.
She never can escape.

MENELAUS

That means delay. Still—if she wants to speak,
she can. I grant her this because of what you say,
not for her sake. She can be sure of that.

HELEN

And perhaps, no matter if you think I speak
the truth or not, you will not talk to me,
since you believe I am your enemy.
Still, I will try to answer what I think
you would say if you spoke your mind,
and my wrongs shall be heard as well as yours.
First: who began these evils? She, the day
when she gave birth to Paris. Who next was guilty?
The old king who decreed the child should live,
and ruined Troy and me—Paris, the hateful,
the firebrand.
What happened then? Listen and learn.
This Paris—he was made the judge for three,
all yoked together in a quarrel—goddesses.
Athena promised he should lead the Trojans
to victory and lay all Greece in ruins.
And Hera said if he thought her the fairest
she would make him lord of Europe and of Asia.
But Aphrodite—well, she praised my beauty—
astonishing, she said—and promised him
that she would give me to him if he judged
that she was loveliest. Then, see what happened.
She won, and so my bridal brought all Greece
great good. No strangers rule you,
no foreign spears, no tyrant.
Oh, it was well for Greece, but not for me,
sold for my beauty and reproached besides
when I deserved a crown.
But—to the point. Is that what you are thinking?
Why did I go—steal from your house in secret?
That man, Paris, or any name you like to call him,

his mother's curse—oh, when he came to me
a mighty goddess walked beside him.
And you, poor fool, you spread your sails for Crete,
left Sparta—left him in your house.
Ah well— Not you, but my own self I ask,
what was there in my heart that I went with him,
a strange man, and forgot my home and country?
Not I, but Aphrodite. Punish her,
be mightier than Zeus who rules
the other gods, but is her slave.
She is my absolution—
One thing with seeming justice you might say.
When Paris died and went down to the grave,
and when no god cared who was in my bed,
I should have left his house—gone to the Greeks.
Just what I tried to do—oh, many times.
I have witnesses—the men who kept the gates,
the watchmen on the walls. Not once, but often
they found me swinging from a parapet,
a rope around this body, stealthily
feeling my way down.
The Trojans then no longer wanted me,
but the man who next took me—and by force—
would never let me go.
My husband, must I die, and at your hands?
You think that right? Is that your justice?
I was forced—by violence. I lived a life
that had no joy, no triumph. In bitterness
I lived a slave.
Do you wish to set yourself above the gods?
Oh, stupid, senseless wish!

A WOMAN

O Queen, defend your children and your country.
Her soft persuasive words are deadly.
She speaks so fair and is so vile.
A fearful thing.

HECUBA

Her goddesses will fight on my side while
I show her for the liar that she is.
Not Hera, not virgin Athena, do I think

would ever stoop to folly great enough
to sell their cities. Hera sell her Argos,
Athena Athens, to be the Trojan's slave!
playing like silly children there on Ida,
and each one in her insolence demanding
the prize for beauty. Beauty—why was Hera
so hot for it? That she might get herself
a better mate than Zeus?
Athena—who so fled from marriage that she begged
one gift from Zeus, virginity.
But she would have the prize, you say. And why?
To help her hunt some god to marry her?
Never make gods out fools to whitewash your own evil.
No one with sense will listen to you.
And Aphrodite, did you say—who would not laugh?
—must take my son to Menelaus' house?
Why? Could she not stay quietly in heaven
and send you on—and all your town—to Troy?
My son was beautiful exceedingly.
You saw him—your own desire was enough.
No need of any goddess.
Men's follies—they are Aphrodite.
She rose up from the sea-foam; where the froth
and foam of life are, there she is.
It was my son. You saw him in his Eastern dress
all bright with gold, and you were mad with love.
Such little things had filled your mind in Argos,
busied with this and that.
Once free of Sparta and in Troy where gold,
you thought, flowed like a river, you would spend
and spend, until your spendthrift hand
had drowned the town.
Your luxuries, your insolent excesses,
Menelaus' halls had grown too small for them.
Enough of that. By force you say he took you?
You cried out? Where? No one in Sparta heard you.
Young Castor was there and his brother too,
not yet among the stars.
And when you came to Troy and on your track the
    Greeks,
and death and agony in battle,

if they would tell you, "Greece has won today,"
you would praise this man here, Menelaus,
to vex my son, who feared him as a rival.
Then Troy had victories, and Menelaus
was nothing to you.
Looking to the successful side—oh yes,
you always followed there.
There was no right or wrong side in your eyes.
And now you talk of ropes—letting your body down
in secret from the wall, longing to go.
Who found you so?
Was there a noose around your neck?
A sharp knife in your hand? Such ways
as any honest woman would have found,
who loved the husband she had lost?
Often and often I would tell you, Go,
my daughter. My sons will find them other wives.
I will help you. I will send you past the lines
to the Greek ships. Oh, end this war
between our foes and us. But this was bitter to you.
In Paris' house you had your insolent way.
You liked to see the Eastern men fall at your feet.
These were great things to you.
Look at the dress you wear, your ornaments.
Is that the way to meet your husband?
You should not dare to breathe the same air with him.
Oh, men should spit upon you.
Humbly, in rags, trembling and shivering,
with shaven head—so you should come,
with shame at last, instead of shamelessness,
for all the wickedness you did.
King, one word more and I am done.
Give Greece a crown, be worthy of yourself.
Kill her. So shall the law stand for all women,
that she who plays false to her husband's bed,
shall die.

A WOMAN

O son of an ancient house, O King, now show
that you are worthy of your fathers.

The Greeks called you a woman, shamed you
with that reproach. Be strong. Be noble. Punish her.

MENELAUS *(impatiently.)*
I see it all as you do. We agree.
She left my house because she wanted to—
went to a stranger's bed. Her talk of Aphrodite—
big words, no more. *(Turns to* HELEN.*)* Go. Death is near.
Men there are awaiting for you. In their hands are stones.
Die—a small price for the Greeks' long suffering.
You shall not any more dishonor me.

HELEN *(kneeling and clinging to him.)*
No! No! Upon my knees—see, I am praying to you.
It was the gods, not me. Oh, do not kill me.
Forgive.

HECUBA
The men she murdered. Think of those
who fought beside you—of their children too.
Never betray them. Hear that prayer.

MENELAUS *(roughly.)*
Enough, old woman. She is nothing to me.
Men, take her to the ships and keep her safe
until she sails.

HECUBA
But not with you! She must not set foot on your ship.

MENELAUS *(bitterly.)*
And why? Her weight too heavy for it?

HECUBA
A lover once, a lover always.

MENELAUS
(pauses a moment to think.)
Not so when what he loved has gone.
But it shall be as you would have it.
Not on the same ship with me. The advice is good.
And when she gets to Argos she shall die
a death hard as her heart.
So in the end she will become a teacher,
teach women chastity—no easy thing,

but yet her utter ruin will strike terror
into their silly hearts,
even women worse than she.

CHORUS

And so your temple in Ilium,
your altar of frankincense,
are given to the Greek,
the flame from the honey, the corn and the oil,
the smoke from the myrrh floating upward,
the holy citadel.
And Ida, the mountain where the ivy grows,
and rivers from the snows rush through the glens,
and the boundary wall of the world
where the first sunlight falls,
the blessed home of the dawn.

The sacrifice is gone, and the glad call
of dancers, and the prayers at evening to the gods
that last the whole night long.
Gone too the golden images,
and the twelve Moons, to Trojans holy.
Do you care, do you care, do you heed these things,
O God, from your throne in high heaven?
My city is perishing,
ending in fire and onrushing flame.

A WOMAN

O dear one, O my husband,
you are dead, and you wander
unburied, uncared for, while over-seas
the ships shall carry me,
swift-winged ships darting onward,
on to the land the riders love,
Argos, where the towers of stone
built by giants reach the sky.

ANOTHER

Children, our children.
At the gate they are crying, crying,
calling to us with tears,
Mother, I am all alone.

They are driving me away
to a black ship, and I cannot see you.

ANOTHER
Where, oh where? To holy Salamis,
with swift oars dipping?
Or to the crest of Corinth,
the city of two seas,
where the gates King Pelops built
for his dwelling stand?

ANOTHER
Oh, if only, far out to sea,
the crashing thunder of God
would fall down, down on Menelaus' ship,
crashing down upon her oars,
the Aegean's wild-fire light.
He it was drove me from Troy.
He is driving me in tears
over to Greece to slavery.

ANOTHER
And Helen, too, with her mirrors of gold,
looking and wondering at herself,
as pleased as a girl.
May she never come to the land of her fathers,
never see the hearth of her home,
her city, the temple with brazen doors
of goddess Athena.
Oh, evil marriage that brought
shame to Greece, the great,
and to the waters of Simois
sorrow and suffering.
   (TALTHYBIUS *approaches with a few soldiers. He is
   carrying the dead child.*)

ANOTHER WOMAN
Before new sufferings are grown old
come other new.
Look, unhappy wives of Troy,
the dead Astyanax.
They threw him from the tower as one might pitch a ball.

Oh, bitter killing.
And now they have him there.

TALTHYBIUS
(he gives the body into HECUBA's *arms.)*
One ship is waiting, Hecuba, to take aboard
the last of all the spoil Achilles' son was given,
and bear it with the measured beat of oars
to Thessaly's high headlands.
The chief himself has sailed because of news
he heard, his father's father
driven from his land by his own son.
So, more for haste even than before,
he went and with him went Andromache.
She drew tears from me there upon the ship
mourning her country, speaking to Hector's grave,
begging a burial for her child, your Hector's son,
who thrown down from the tower lost his life.
And this bronze-fronted shield, the dread of many a
    Greek,
which Hector used in battle,
that it should never, so she prayed,
hang in strange halls, her grief before her eyes,
nor in that bridal chamber where she must be a wife,
Andromache, this dead boy's mother.
She begged that he might lie upon it in his grave,
instead of cedar wood or vault of stone.
And in your arms she told me I must lay him,
for you to cover the body, if you still
have anything, a cloak left—
And to put flowers on him if you could,
since she has gone. Her master's haste
kept her from burying her child.
So now, whenever you have laid him out,
we'll heap the earth above him, then
up with the sails!
Do all as quickly as you can. One trouble
I saved you. When we passed Scamander's stream
I let the water run on him and washed his wounds.
I am off to dig his grave now, break up the hard earth.

Working together, you and I,
will hurry to the goal, oars swift for home.

HECUBA

Set the shield down—the great round shield of Hector.
I wish I need not look at it.
 (TALTHYBIUS *goes out with the soldiers.*)
You Greeks, your spears are sharp but not your wits.
You feared a child. You murdered him.
Strange murder. You were frightened, then? You thought
he might build up our ruined Troy? And yet
when Hector fought and thousands at his side,
we fell beneath you. Now, when all is lost,
the city captured and the Trojans dead,
a little child like this made you afraid.
The fear that comes when reason goes away—
Myself, I do not wish to share it.
 (*She dismisses the Greeks and their ways.*)
Beloved, what a death has come to you.
If you had fallen fighting for the city,
if you had known strong youth and love
and godlike power, if we could think
you had known happiness—if there is
happiness anywhere—
But now—you saw and knew, but with your soul
you did not know, and what was in your house
you could not use.
Poor little one. How savagely our ancient walls,
Apollo's towers, have torn away the curls
your mother's fingers wound and where she pressed
her kisses—here where the broken bone grins white—
Oh no—I cannot—
Dear hands, the same dear shape your father's had,
how loosely now you fall. And dear proud lips
forever closed. False words you spoke to me
when you would jump into my bed, call me sweet names
and tell me, Grandmother, when you are dead,
I'll cut off a great lock of hair and lead my soldiers all
to ride out past your tomb.
Not you, but I, old, homeless, childless,
must lay you in your grave, so young,

so miserably dead.
Dear God. How you would run to greet me.
And I would nurse you in my arms, and oh,
so sweet to watch you sleep. All gone.
What could a poet carve upon your tomb?
"A child lies here whom the Greeks feared and slew."
Ah, Greece should boast of that.
Child, they have taken all that was your father's,
but one thing, for your burying, you shall have,
the bronze-barred shield.
It kept safe Hector's mighty arm, but now
it has lost its master.
The grip of his own hand has marked it—dear to me then—
His sweat has stained the rim. Often and often
in battle it rolled down from brows and beard
while Hector held the shield close.
Come, bring such covering for the pitiful dead body
as we still have. God has not left us much
to make a show with. Everything I have
I give you, child.
    O men, secure when once good fortune comes—
fools, fools. Fortune's ways—
here now, there now. She springs
away—back—and away, an idiot's dance.
No one is ever always fortunate.
    (*The women have come in with coverings and gar-
    lands.*)

A WOMAN

Here, for your hands, they bring you clothing for the
    dead,
got from the spoils of Troy.

HECUBA
(*shrouding the body and putting garlands beside it.*)
Oh, not because you conquered when the horses raced,
or with the bow outdid your comrades,
your father's mother lays these wreaths beside you,
and of all that was yours, gives you this covering.
A woman whom God hates has robbed you,
taken your life, when she had taken your treasure
and ruined all your house.

A WOMAN

Oh, my heart! As if you touched it—touched it.
Oh, this was once our prince, great in the city.

HECUBA

So on your wedding day I would have dressed you,
the highest princess of the East your bride.
Now on your body I must lay the raiment,
all that is left of the splendor that was Troy's.
And the dear shield of Hector, glorious in battle,
mother of ten thousand triumphs won,
it too shall have its wreath of honor,
undying it will lie beside the dead.
More honorable by far than all the armor
Odysseus won, the wicked and the wise.

A WOMAN

You, O child, our bitter sorrow,
earth will now receive.
Mourn, O Mother.

HECUBA

Mourn, indeed.

A WOMAN

Weeping for all the dead.

HECUBA

Bitter tears.

A WOMAN

Your sorrows that can never be forgotten.
  (*The funeral rite is now begun,* HECUBA *symbolically
  healing the wounds.*)

HECUBA

I heal your wounds; with linen I bind them.
Ah, in words only, not in truth—
a poor physician.
But soon among the dead your father
will care for you.

A WOMAN

Beat, beat your head.

Lift your hands and let them fall,
moving in measure.

HECUBA

O Women. Dearest—

A WOMAN

Oh, speak to us. Your cry—what does it mean?

HECUBA

Only this the gods would have,
pain for me and pain for Troy,
those they hated bitterly.
Vain, vain, the bulls we slew.
And yet—had God not bowed us down,
not laid us low in dust,
none would have sung of us or told our wrongs
in stories men will listen to forever.
Go: lay our dead in his poor grave,
with these last gifts of death given to him.
I think those that are gone care little
how they are buried. It is we, the living,
our vanity.

*(Women lift the shield with the body on it and carry
it out.)*

A WOMAN

Poor mother—her high hopes were stayed on you
and they are broken.
They called you happy at your birth,
a good man's son.
Your death was miserable exceedingly.

ANOTHER

Oh, see, see—
On the crested height of Troy
fiery hands. They are flinging torches.
Can it be
some new evil?
Something still unknown?

TALTHYBIUS

(stops as he enters and speaks off stage.)
Captains, attention. You have been given charge

to burn this city. Do not let your torches sleep.
Hurry the fire on.
When once the town is level with the ground
then off for home and glad goodbye to Troy.
And you, you Women—I will arrange for you
as well, one speech for everything—
whenever a loud trumpet-call is sounded,
go to the Greek ships, to embark.
Old woman, I am sorriest for you,
follow. Odysseus' men are here to get you.
He drew you—you must leave here as his slave.

HECUBA

The end then. Well—the height of sorrow, I stand there.
Troy is burning—I am going.
But—hurry, old feet, if you can,
a little nearer—here, where I can see
my poor town, say goodbye to her.
You were so proud a city, in all the East
the proudest. Soon your name the whole world knew,
will be taken from you. They are burning you
and leading us away, their slaves.
O God— What makes me say that word?
The gods— I prayed, they never listened.
Quick, into the fire— Troy, I will die with you.
Death then—oh, beautiful.

TALTHYBIUS

Out of your head, poor thing, with all you've suffered.
Lead her away— Hold her, don't be too gentle.
She must be taken to Odysseus.
Give her into his hands. She is his—
    (Shakes his head.)
his prize.
    (It grows darker.)

A WOMAN

Ancient of days, our country's Lord,
Father, who made us,
You see your children's sufferings.
Have we deserved them?

ANOTHER

He sees—but Troy has perished, the great city.
No city now, never again.

ANOTHER

Oh, terrible!
The fire lights the whole town up.
The inside rooms are burning.
The citadel—it is all flame now.

ANOTHER

Troy is vanishing.
War first ruined her.
And what was left is rushing up in smoke,
the glorious houses fallen.
First the spear and then the fire.

HECUBA

*(She stands up and seems to be calling to someone far
away.)*
Children, hear, your mother is calling.

A WOMAN *(gently.)*
They are dead, those you are speaking to.

HECUBA

My knees are stiff, but I must kneel.
Now, strike the ground with both my hands—

A WOMAN

I too, I kneel upon the ground.
I call to mine down there.
Husband, poor husband.

HECUBA

They are driving us like cattle—taking us away.

A WOMAN

Pain, all pain.

ANOTHER

To a slave's house, from my country.

HECUBA

Priam, Priam, you are dead,
and not a friend to bury you.

The evil that has found me—
do you know?

A WOMAN

No. Death has darkened his eyes.
He was good and the wicked killed him.

HECUBA

O dwellings of the gods and O dear city,
the spear came first and now
only the red flame lives there.

A WOMAN

Fall and be forgotten. Earth is kind.

ANOTHER

The dust is rising, spreading out like a great wing of
    smoke.
I cannot see my house.

ANOTHER

The name has vanished from the land,
and we are gone, one here, one there.
And Troy is gone forever.
    (*A great crash is heard.*)

HECUBA

Did you hear? Did you know—

A WOMAN

The fall of Troy—

ANOTHER

Earthquake and flood and the city's end—

HECUBA

Trembling body—old weak limbs,
you must carry me on to the new day of slavery.
    (*A trumpet sounds.*)

A WOMAN

Farewell, dear city.
Farewell, my country, where once my children lived.
On to the ships—
There below, the Greek ships wait.
    (*The trumpet sounds again and the women pass out.*)

THE STRENGTH OF MANKIND HAS ALWAYS BEEN ITS WOMEN

KATHARINE HEPBURN
AS
HECUBA
VANESSA REDGRAVE
AS
ANDROMACHE
GENEVIEVE BUJOLD
AS
CASSANDRA
IRENE PAPAS
AS
HELEN

"THE
TROJAN
WOMEN"

BASED UPON THE EDITH HAMILTON
TRANSLATION OF THE PLAY BY EURIPIDES
SCREENPLAY BY
MICHAEL CACOYANNIS

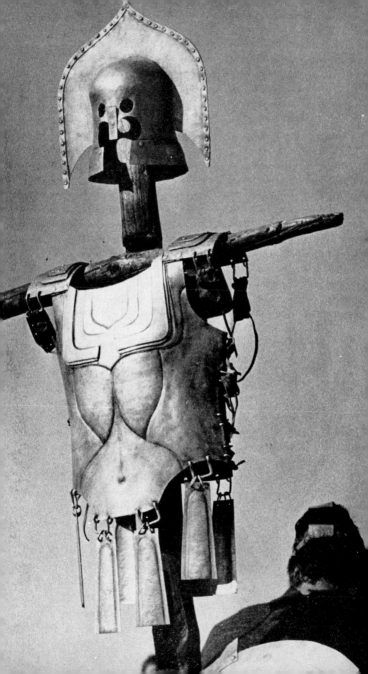

"THE TROJAN WOMEN"

Screenplay
by
MICHAEL CACOYANNIS

Based upon the
Edith Hamilton
Translation of the
Play by Euripides

DIRECTOR'S NOTE

Whenever people talk of classical drama, I detect that ring of reverence in their voice that is reserved for the sacrosanct and the very old. It must make the poor authors turn in their graves. Surely, the essence of all great works lies in their triumph over time. Any approach that puts the emphasis on age rather than on agelessness can only diminish their impact by creating a false sense of distance between them and us.

The Greek plays, by virtue of their seniority, have suffered the longest and most from this approach, starting with the plodding, pedantic translations stuffed down our throats at school, down to those stage productions that one can only describe as parodies of academic reproduction.

It took me years—and I am not ashamed to admit it—to get past this barrier of respect and uninvolvement. Suddenly, I discovered Euripides. His *Electra* (a play that has been unfairly neglected because of scholarly disapproval) fell accidentally into my hands and I read it for the first time. Out of this, for me extraordinary encounter, grew a film and an association with a great author which has gone on ever since.

The stage production of *The Trojan Women* was next. This was a play I knew but whose full impact had escaped me until 1964 when I read Edith Hamilton's masterly translation. Masterly because it succeeds in recreating the rhythmic structure of the original without imprisoning it in the poetic style of some other age—Elizabethan, Victorian or idiomatic modern—and with a clarity that continually illuminates it in depth. I've thanked her and loved her for it ever since. And I regret that she was never able to see the way American audiences responded when, later that same year, I staged the play at the Circle-in-the-Square in New York.

There have been many changes in my life since then. The most important resulted from the take-over by a military regime in Greece, with all the repressions that such an event implies. Like many other Greek artists, I made the one free choice open to me. Not to surrender that freedom of expression which is every man's birthright, but to go on exercising it from countries other than my own. The need, stronger now than it had ever been before, to cry out against oppression in any shape, place or form, found its release, once again, through the words of my favorite author.

Directing his *Iphigenia in Aulis* in New York, a play that rips open the festering evils of political and military ambition, I became convinced that, through sheer emotional impact, Euripides is as challenging to contemporary conscience as any author living today.

This conviction, and my growing horror at the massive crimes being committed in the name of political causes culminated in my decision to transpose *The Trojan Women* to the screen. Appalled by the Melos massacre of 416 B.C., Euripides used the Trojan wars to hold up the mirror to his own people. Twenty-four hundred years later, the mirror is as clear and as accusing to the contemporary image as ever.

The timing seemed right on another level. I felt that I now had gained enough distance from the stage production to approach the material from a purely cinematic viewpoint. To succeed in lifting it out of the bastard status of "filmed theater," and integrate the text into the visual reality of cinema in the most economical and emotionally effective way possible. There was no guilt involved in cutting or transposing words. It has always seemed to me more important to respect the spirit rather than the letter of an author's intentions.

What is extraordinary in Euripides is his technique of opening up the action to establish a dramatic situation and then focusing in on his characters at such close range that you feel you are looking straight into their souls. It is a technique so visually dynamic as to convince me that if he were alive today, film would be his favorite medium. Not only as a means of expression, but as a way of reaching the widest possible public, like that which flocked to see his plays in ancient Athens.

Whenever I can, I like to cast a film before I attack the script. Investing the characters with an identity gives me a dimension of reality that helps to stimulate my imagination. In the case of *The Trojan Women*, precasting was an artistic necessity. There was no wavering in my choice of the four actresses. I made it as much on the basis of their talent as for their very special qualities as human beings, their outlook, their spirit. This spirit, and especially Katharine Hepburn's, who was the first to rally and the last to leave the location, not only made the film possible but radiates through their performances in a manner that makes the difficult art of acting seem as natural as breathing.

MICHAEL CACOYANNIS

Paris
May, 1971

It is night ... On the sound track, confused at first and gradually swelling till it dominates, we hear a veritable caldron of women's voices, rising in waves of grief and terror. The credits appear over swirling smoke and dust.

Camera pulls back to reveal a crowd of women being herded like cattle. Some of them hold terrified children, others look desperately around, searching, others hide their faces. Harsh male voices shouting orders are heard above the confusion.

Women being dragged out of homes and churches.

Women being separated from their children.

Women being stripped of their jewelry and other possessions.

Children being led away in droves.

Plunder moving past, piled high on carts, on horses, on men's backs—a shimmering stream of the city's treasures.

Over the above, a voice:

> VOICE
>
> Ten years—
> ten times the seed was sown before Troy fell,
> perished beneath Greek spears.
> *(Pause)*
> A desert now where homes were. Blood
> drips down from the holy shrines.
> While to the Greek ships pass the Trojan treasure,
> gold, gold in masses, armor, clothing
> stripped from the dead.
> *(Pause)*
> O fools! The men who lay a city waste,
> so soon to die themselves.

We are now outside the massive city walls. Soldiers carrying torches guide the torrent of women out of the gates and along a huge dried-up ditch.

In the shadow of the looming walls, a fenced area of scorched waste ground serving as the women's camp. The women are being maneuvered into enclosures. As they file past, soldiers stamp numbers into their arms with dented seals that cut into the flesh.

VOICE

Scamander's stream is loud with lamentation,
so many captive women weeping.
Their masters drew lots for them. Some will go
to Arcady and some to Thessaly.
Some to the lords of Athens, Theseus' sons.

A complex of wooden huts and tents at the foot of the walls. Several carts drive up loaded with women, the noble ones. They are taken down and directed toward the huts.

VOICE

Huts here hold others spared the lot,
but chosen for the great captains.
With them, like them a captive of the spear,
the Spartan woman, Helen.

There is a burst of shrill, angry voices.

The women in and around the enclosures yell curses and stir dangerously. Fearing a stampede, the soldiers attack with characteristic brutality. As the women fall back stumbling, screaming, the camera swings away and discovers the object of their fury. Helen, cloaked, standing erect on a cart being driven toward the huts, guarded by several soldiers.

Camera wanders over the scene of desolation and terror, highlighted here and there by the open fires lit by the Greeks. The women's wailing is now muffled, like moaning wind. A sentry paces outside the huts holding a torch. We catch a glimpse of the women, still and silent like ghosts.

VOICE

But if a man would look on misery,
it is here to see.

The flickering light of the torch falls on a woman crumpled up on the stony ground under the walls. The soldier lingers.

VOICE

Hecuba lies there
outside the gates.

The soldier moves on and the crumpled figure is swallowed
up by the darkness.

VOICE

Gone is her husband, gone her sons,
all dead.

Dawn. Gray and silent. A pall of smoke and mist hangs over
the women's camp. On the top of the walls a guard. Camera
pans down and centers on the motionless body of the woman
—Hecuba, the Trojan queen—still on the ground. It tracks in
slowly. She stirs. Her voice seems to grow out of the earth of
which she is part.

HECUBA

Up.
Up from the ground,
O weary head, breaking neck.

Her hand now feels the harsh surface of the stone wall. Her
head is still down.

HECUBA

This is no longer Troy. And we are not
the lords of Troy.
Endure. The ways of fate are the ways of the wind.
Drift with the stream—drift with fate.

Slowly, painfully, she props herself up into a crouching posi-
tion against the wall. Her head swings to one side and we see
the ravaged face beyond pain.

HECUBA

All was nothing, nothing always.
Keep silent? Speak?
Weep then? Why? For what?
Oh . . .
This aching body—this bed—
it is very hard.
Up! Quick, quick, I must move.

With sudden energy she gets to her feet. She staggers a few
steps, then stops. Sounds of stifled moaning are heard from
the direction of the tents.

HECUBA

Oh I'll rock myself this way, that way,

to the sound of weeping, the song of tears
dropping down forever.

She closes her eyes, her body swaying.

HECUBA

O Greeks! Out from your fair bays and harbors,
over the dark shining sea,
you found your way to our holy city,
and the fearful music of war was heard.

Some horses ride past, raising dust. Her eyes flash with anger.
She cries out defiantly, with gathering rage.

HECUBA

What did you come for? A woman?
A thing of loathing, of shame.
She slew Priam, the king,
father of fifty sons,
she wrecked me upon the reef of destruction.

Hearing Hecuba's cry, the women peer out of the huts. One
after another they steal out, gripped with terror.

HECUBA

(Cries out)
Who am I
that I wait here—
a Greek king's slave,
shaven head brought low in dishonor.

She turns to the women.

HECUBA

O wives of the bronze-armored men who fought
and young girls plighted to shame ... See—
only smoke left where was Troy.

The women move in closer.

HEBUCA

Let us weep for her.

Gradually their voices are released and build up into one
anguished, confused cry. More women burst out of the huts
and arrive running. Camera moves among them, catching odd
phrases, as the terrified faces loom in the foreground.

WOMAN 1

(Running up)
Your cry, Hecuba, what does it mean?

WOMAN 2

What will they do? Carry us off
in a ship far from home?

HECUBA

You ask and I know nothing.
Except that ruin is here.

WOMAN 3

Not death—they would not think of death . . .

HECUBA

Look, there where the Greek ships lie—

Some women help two young girls to climb up on a high rock.

GIRL 1

The sailors—
they're standing on the prow.

A wave of panic goes through the women.

GIRL 1

They're running out the oars—

WOMAN 2

We shall hear the summons.
Women of Troy, go forth, for the Greeks set sail.

WOMAN 1

A Greek's bed—oh no,
not that for me . . .

WOMAN 4

Whose slave shall I be?

WOMEN

Whose slave I? Where? Argos? Phthia?

HECUBA

(Bursting through with defiant rage)
And I? A slave? to whom? Where—how?
I watch a master's door?

I nurse his children?
Once I was queen of Troy.

The women fall silent.

GIRL 2

Look.

GIRL 1

A herald.

GIRL 2

Something has happened.
He comes so fast.

The two girls climb down quickly. The women fall in behind
the queen. In the silence she speaks in a low voice, as if in
prayer.

HECUBA

Not Cassandra—no, not her.
She is mad—she has been driven mad.
   (To the women)
Keep her within.
Not shamed before the Greeks—not that grief too.

The women run off toward Cassandra's hut.

The herald, a tall, tough soldier in his middle thirties, rides
up followed by some horsemen. He looks at the women in
silence.

TALTHYBIUS

You know me, Hecuba. I have often come
with messages to Troy from the Greek camp.
Talthybius.

He dismounts.

She looks at him without moving.

TALTHYBIUS

I bring you news.

HECUBA

It has come, women of Troy. Once we
only feared it.

TALTHYBIUS

The lots are drawn, if that is what
you feared.

HECUBA

Lots?

TALTHYBIUS

A different man takes each.
You're not to go together.

HECUBA

Which takes which?

WOMEN

Who? Where? Thessaly? Phthia? Thebes?

TALTHYBIUS

(Abruptly)
Not all at once!

A hush falls.

HECUBA

My daughter, who—who drew her? Tell me—
Cassandra—

TALTHYBIUS

King Agamemnon chose her out from all.

A pause.

HECUBA

Aah! To serve his Spartan wife?

TALTHYBIUS

No, no—he chose her for himself.

HECUBA

Never. She took a sacred vow to God for all her life.
She is his, a virgin, always.

TALTHYBIUS

He loved her for that same strange purity.

She has no weapon to fight him. She just stares.

TALTHYBIUS

Well, now—a king's bed is not so bad.

A pause.

HECUBA

My other child you took from me last night.

TALTHYBIUS

(Cagily)
Polyxena, you mean?

HECUBA

Her. Who drew her?

TALTHYBIUS

They led her off to watch Achilles' tomb.

HECUBA

To watch a tomb? My daughter?
What strange ritual is that, my friend?

TALTHYBIUS

(Embarrassed, evading)
Just think of her as happy—and be glad.

HECUBA

(Uneasy)
Why do you speak like that?
She is alive?

TALTHYBIUS

(Somehow unable to tell her)
What happened was—
well, she is free from trouble.

Hecuba looks around with large, questioning eyes, somehow afraid to pursue the matter further. The women have realized but say nothing.

Three large carts filled with soldiers drive up just inside the camp. They wait in readiness.

Hecuba stiffens and goes on.

HECUBA

And Hector's wife—my Hector—
Andromache?

TALTHYBIUS

Achilles' son took her.

HECUBA

Where is she?

TALTHYBIUS

In Greek hands.
Caught while trying to escape with her son.

A short pause.

HECUBA

And I, old gray head, whose am I?

TALTHYBIUS

Slave of the king of Ithaca, Odysseus.

Her pent-up despair explodes.

HECUBA

Beat, beat my head! Tear, tear my cheek!
His slave—vile lying man. I have come to this—
There's nothing good he does not hurt—a lawless beast.
A double tongue as false in hate, as false in love.
Pity me, women of Troy,
I am gone—I am lost—O wretched!

Infected by the violence of her outburst, the women go ber-
serk. They break their ranks and spring around Talthybius,
shouting.

WOMEN

And I? Who takes me?
Where do I go? What man owns me?

Talthybius backs, yells an order, and the soldiers jump off the
carts. After some struggle they reestablish order. A heavy
silence reigns. Talthybius, a simple man whose basic humanity
is at odds with his mission, walks the length of the line of
women held back by the soldiers, looking at them gruffly. He
steps near a soldier.

TALTHYBIUS

Bring Cassandra here.

The soldier looks at him, not knowing where to go. Talthybius
turns to the women.

TALTHYBIUS

Where?

The women do not speak. They keep staring at Hecuba.
Talthybius orders some soldiers to follow him and marches
off toward the huts. Hecuba follows with her eyes, then

tentatively moves after them, knowing they will find her, wanting to be close when they do.

TALTHYBIUS
(Shouting to the soldiers)
Be quick. King Agamemnon's waiting.
We must take her to his ship
and then these here,
to all the other generals.

The soldiers shout to any women still in the huts to come out. The few that were hiding creep out. Hecuba is still approaching slowly. The two women who had gone off to look after Cassandra run past, their huge eyes offering mute apologies of fear, but Hecuba is not involved. She is a mother, all compassion, there to help the mentally disturbed child who has a special place in her heart. The huts are empty. And now the soldiers start rushing in with their spears or tearing down the more improvised structures.

Smoke goes up through the cracks of one of the huts. And a flame can be seen moving inside. Hecuba gasps. She accelerates toward the hut.

The soldiers guarding the women notice. One of them breaks into a run, shouting to warn Talthybius.

GUARD
Fire! Over there!

Talthybius sees and starts running, followed by several soldiers. Meanwhile, some women who have been lurking about, hearing the cry "Fire" are gripped by a frenzy of self-destruction. They start running toward the hut screaming, "We'll burn ourselves alive . . . all of us . . ."

Talthybius yells an order and the soldiers go after them. Before they can reach the hut they grab them and drag them away violently.

Hecuba stops in the doorway of the hut as Talthybius arrives running. She half-turns and says quietly:

HECUBA
There is nothing burning.
It is my daughter Cassandra.
She is mad.

Inside the hut, smoke is thick. Cassandra, dressed like a
priestess (not unlike a nun's habit), is moving around a pyre
as if involved in some strange ritual. The flame leaps dangerously up to the roof. She holds a torch and speaks in the
monotonous voice used in religious incantation.

CASSANDRA

I praise him. I bear a flame.
With my torch I touch to fire
this holy place.
Blessed the bridegroom,
blessed am I
to lie with a king in a king's bed in Argos.

Torn, Hecuba moves toward the demented girl. Cassandra
looks at her closely.

CASSANDRA

Mother, you weep
tears for the beloved country lost.
I for my bridal here
lift up the fire's flame
to the dawn, to the splendor,
to you, O Hymen.

She lifts her torch dangerously. Her mother tries to restrain
her, but Cassandra slips away wildly, dancing around the hut.

CASSANDRA

Fly dancing feet,
Up with the dance.
Oh joy, oh joy!
Dance for my father dead,
most blessed to die.

The roof has caught fire. Hecuba cries out. In a leap Talthybius and the soldiers are inside putting out the fire, yelling
and cursing. Cassandra runs out.

The sun is rising yellow and sickly through the drifting
smoke. A soldier's silhouette is outlined dimly. Cassandra
slows down. Her eyes are filled with wonder.

CASSANDRA

Apollo—you?
There in the laurel grove
I served your altar.

The soldier moves toward her—the spell is broken. She turns away and runs up to her mother who has followed her outside.

CASSANDRA

Dance, mother, come.
Keep step with me.
Sing—
Sing to the marriage god.

She begins to sing in a heartbreaking, discordant voice. Suddenly breaks off. Yells.

CASSANDRA

Sing for the bride.
Joyously. ALL.

Silence. She looks around her wildly and runs off. Talthybius and the men go after her.

Camera is infected by the girl's frenzy as she runs toward the women.

CASSANDRA

(Shouting)
Women of Troy,
dressed in your best,
honor my marriage,
honor him too,
whose bed fate drives me to share.

She bolts away once again. Two soldiers block her way with their spears. She backs against the wall, holding the torch in front of her, moving it dangerously. The soldiers are about to close in on her but Hecuba stops them. Carefully, measuring every move, she approaches Cassandra.

HECUBA

(Gently)
Child . . .

Cassandra looks at her, without moving.

HECUBA

Give me your torch.

Cassandra moves the torch out of her reach.

HECUBA

You do not hold it straight,
you move so wildly.
Your sufferings, my child,
have never taught you wisdom.

Cassandra grows quiet, passive. Hecuba takes the torch, holds
it out toward the women.

HECUBA

Here! Someone take it.

A woman runs up and takes it from her.

HECUBA

This marriage needs no songs,
but only tears.

Weary, heartbroken, she avoids looking at Cassandra, who
seems overcome by a strange calm. When Cassandra raises
her eyes, they are clear, full of wisdom. She speaks in a
quiet, deeply compassionate voice.

CASSANDRA

O mother, crown my triumph with a wreath.
Be glad, for I am married to a king.
Send me to him. And if I shrink away,
drive me with violence. If God still lives,
my marriage shall be bloodier than Helen's.
Agamemnon the great, the glorious lord of Greece,
I shall kill him, mother, lay his house as low
as he laid ours, make him pay for all
he made my father suffer, brothers, and—
But no. I must not speak of that—that ax
which on my neck—on others' too—
nor of that murder of a mother
by her own children—

Her eyes seem to be looking into the future with growing
horror. Unable to decipher her words, disturbed, afraid for
her, Hecuba tries to break the spell. Cassandra looks at her
for a long moment, then takes her hand and turns her gently
toward Troy.

CASSANDRA

I will show you.

This town, yes, mother,
is happier than the Greeks.

This is more than Hecuba can stand. She turns away, but
Cassandra holds her fast.

CASSANDRA

I know that I am mad,
but mother dearest, now, for this one time,
I do not rave.

Her voice carries such conviction that Hecuba and all the
women turn and look at her, listening.

CASSANDRA

One woman they came hunting
and men by tens of thousands died.
And why? She had fled because she wished,
not forced to go. No man attacked their borders
or laid siege to their high-walled towns.
But those whom war took never saw their children.
No wife with gentle hands shrouded them
    for their grave.
They lie in a strange land. And in their homes
are sorrows too, the very same.
Lonely women who died, old men who waited
for sons that never came . . .

Silence. Even Talthybius seems to be under the spell. She
looks at him.

CASSANDRA

That was the glorious victory they won.

The women gasp. She turns to her mother.

CASSANDRA

But we—we Trojans died to save our people,
no glory greater. All those the Greeks slew,
friends bore them home. The earth of their own land
covered them. The rest, through the long
    days they fought,
had wife and child at hand, not like the Greeks,
whose joys were far away,
And Hector's pain—your Hector . . .

At the mention of her dead son's name Hecuba turns away in
pain.

CASSANDRA

Mother, hear me.
This is the truth: he died the best, a hero.
Because the Greeks came, he died thus.
Had they stayed home, we never would
    have known him.
This truth stands firm: the wise will fly from war.
But if war comes, to die well is to win
a victor's crown.
So, mother, do not pity Troy,
or me—upon my bridal bed.

Mother and daughter cling to each other, suddenly isolated
from the reality around them by their love for each other.
Talthybius feels the need to assert his authority.

TALTHYBIUS

(Gruffly)
Now if God hadn't made her mad,
I would have paid her for those evil words,
bad omens, and my general sailing soon.

He strides up to the two women. Hecuba looks up and is
shocked back to the dreadful reality. Cassandra doesn't turn.

TALTHYBIUS

(To Cassandra)
Now you—you know your mind's not quite right.
So all you said against Greece I never heard.
The wind blew it away.
Come with me to the ship now.

Cassandra turns and looks at him as if for the first time.

CASSANDRA

(Haughtily)
A strange sort of slave, surely.
Messengers I think such men are called,
    envoys, spokesmen,
hated by all, for they are tyrants' tools.

He grabs her by the arm and pulls her away. Hecuba is ready
to run after her, but he blocks her way.

TALTHYBIUS

And you, do follow quietly when Odysseus' men come.
His wife's a good wise woman, so they say.

He turns and goes after Cassandra, who walks steadily ahead.
He lingers by a group of soldiers.

TALTHYBIUS
(*Mumbling*)
A grand match for our general, she is.

The soldiers laugh.

SOLDIER
Well, I'm a poor man,
but I'd not go to bed with her.

He gives the soldiers some silent orders. They fan out toward
the enclosures, shouting out numbers.

The scene becomes noisy again, confused. Cassandra stops,
disturbed, shaking. She shouts at Talthybius.

CASSANDRA
Come, let us hasten to my marriage.
We two shall rest, the bridegroom, and the bride,
within the house of death.

Talthybius grabs her violently and lifts her on to one of the
waiting carts. She looks around wildly.

Women are being led or dragged on to the other carts. They
cling to each other, shouting good-bye to the other women.

WOMAN
(*Shouting*)
My dead sons.
I would look at them once more.

The sound of wailing swells. The horses grow restless.
Cassandra blocks her ears, her frenzy mounting.

CASSANDRA
O Greek king, with your dreams of grandeur
    yet to come,
vile as you are, so shall your end be,
in darkness—all light gone.
And me—a cleft in the hills,
washed by winter rains,
his tomb nearby.
There—dead—cast out—naked—

and wild beasts seeking food—
it is I there—I myself—Apollo's servant.

A shout goes up among the women left behind. "Sing . . .
sing." As if to drown the terror, a song starts, getting louder
and louder. Desperate eyes, desperate voices, offering comfort
to those taken away first.

Talthybius jumps on to the cart next to Cassandra. He looks
at her almost in fear. She tears at her clothes, ripping them
off.

CASSANDRA

Off; Sacred veils, mysterious wreaths,
away, I tear them from my neck.
My flesh still clean, I give them back to you.

The carriage starts jerkily. She grabs the rail.

CASSANDRA

Spread the sail. The wind comes swift.

As the carriage gathers speed, the wind ruffles her hair,
tumbling loosely around her bare shoulders. Camera tracks
close to her.

CASSANDRA

(Looking toward the camp)
Mother, my mother, do not weep.

She looks around at the landscape rushing past.

CASSANDRA

Farewell, dear city.

She kneels by the rail, looking at the dusty soil.

CASSANDRA

Brothers, in Troy's earth laid, my father,
a little time and I am with you.

Slowly she raises her eyes, streaming with proud tears, looking back at her mother for the last time.

Hecuba in the distance, growing tinier and tinier as the cart
drives on.

Hecuba's eyes are fixed on the disappearing cart. She takes a
few meaningless steps in its direction. Suddenly she sways
and falls to the ground.

WOMAN 1

The queen!

Several women run up to her. As they bend down to lift her up Hecuba's voice stops them.

HECUBA

Let me be. Kindness not wanted is unkindness.
I cannot stand. Too much is on me.

The women back away, forming a circle of compassion around her.

HECUBA

O God— Do I call to you? You did not help.

She makes an effort to pull herself together, sits up, her eyes flashing with the defiance of someone who doesn't want to spare herself any grief, however terrible.

HECUBA

Oh, I will think of days gone,
days to make a song of,
crowning my sorrow by remembering.
We were kings and a king I married.
Sons I bore him, many sons.
That means little—but fine, brave lads.
No woman, Trojan, Greek, or stranger,
had sons like mine to be proud of.
I saw them fall beneath Greek spears.
Their father—I did not learn from others
that I must weep for him—these eyes beheld him,
I, my own self, saw him fall, murdered.
My daughters, maidens reared to marry kings,
are torn from me. For the Greeks I reared them.

A pause. The soldiers look on.

HECUBA

And now the end.
An old gray slave woman I go to Greece.
The door to shut and open, bowing low
—I, who bore Hector—torn rags around me,
torn flesh beneath.

Her mind seems to wander. Her voice grows small, almost childlike.

HECUBA
Daughter, who knew God's mystery and joy,
what strange chance lost you your virginity?
Polyxena, where are you gone?

Her voice trails off. Some women run up and lift her up. She doesn't resist.

HECUBA
Why lift me up? What hope is there to hold to?

She turns and starts to walk away among the women, who make way reverently.

HECUBA
Count no one happy, however fortunate,
before he dies.

A strange calm dominates—a respite from terror and a return to dignity. Hecuba stops in the shade of an old tree and stands there, immobile, her eyes lost in time.

Camera wanders among the women. The silence is accentuated by the distant sound of drums from the Greek camp. One senses their emotional unity as the current of their thoughts flows back to the dreadful event that changed their lives so inexorably. Their eyes—huge, in close-up—look straight into the camera and the words come from that inner compulsion that makes people relate the events of some tragedy over and over.

WOMAN 5
A four-wheeled cart brought the wooden
horse to the gates.
Gold was the rein and the bridle ...

WOMAN 6
Deadly the arms within.

WOMAN 7
High on Troy's rock the people cried,
"Rest at last, trouble ended.
Bring the carven image in,
fit gift to God who gave us peace."

WOMAN 8
Who of the young but hurried forth?

WOMAN 9
Who of the old would stay at home?

WOMAN 10
With song and rejoicing
we hastened to the gate,
to that smooth-planed horse of wood
where the Greeks were hiding . . .

WOMAN 6
Where was Troy's destruction.

WOMEN
With ropes of twisted flax,
as a ship's dark hull is drawn to land,
we brought it to the temple of stone,
through streets that soon would run with blood . . .

WOMAN 5
And we were singing . . .

A pause. The memory of that short-lived happiness holds
them in its bitter thrall.

WOMAN 9
The dark of evening fell
and still the lutes rang out
to the songs of Troy.
The houses blazed with light
and sleep was not.

Another pause. The faces darken. The images of horror attack
like evil birds. Memory of pain so fresh becomes reality re-
lived. The sounds of war—so familiar to generations of men—
burst through, mingling with the women's cries.

WOMAN 6
A shout rang out in the town . . .

WOMAN 7
A cry of blood through the houses . . .

WOMAN 8
And a frightened child caught his mother's skirt
and hid himself in her cloak.

WOMEN
Then war came forth from his hiding place—
the God-fearing Greeks had devised it.

WOMAN 9
Around the altars they slaughtered us . . .

WOMAN 10
Within on their beds lay headless men . . .

WOMAN 11
Young men cut down in their prime.

The apprehensive soldiers start breaking them up. The women
look at them defiantly.

WOMAN 5
(Shouting)
That was the triumph crown of Greece.

GIRL
We shall bear children for them to rear,
grief and shame to our country.

A deserted landscape near the sea. Charred trees and wreck-
age of battle. Here and there, mounds of earth mark the
graves of the fallen. A horse-drawn chariot with a man's
glittering armor raised on a wooden cross clatters up and
stops. A little boy of three is raised on to it and stands there,
tiny in front of the ghostlike panoply, looking out.

Through the shimmering smoke of incense burning on
Achilles' grave—surrounded by large blocks of stone—we see
a tall beautiful woman approaching, followed by two armed
soldiers. She walks with a steady step, upright, unseeing. At
the grave, a guard hands her a wreath. He silently orders her
to kneel. Only then does she see and her face twitches with
pain. A girl's body lies face down among the stones, her hair
streaming around her shoulders.

ANDROMACHE
(Whispering)
Polyxena . . .

She takes off her cloak and covers the girl's naked body. Then,
rising quickly, she follows the soldiers to the chariot. She
looks at the armor in voiceless grief and tenderness.
Brusquely, one of the soldiers lifts her up next to her son,
while the other soldier climbs up next to the driver. The
chariot moves off noisily.

The women's camp. Two women run up to some others, pointing off.

WOMAN 2
Look, it's Andromache.

WOMAN 12
And with her dear Astyanax,
the son of Hector.

More women join them and together they move off in the direction of the approaching chariot. One woman runs up to Hecuba, who still stands by the olive tree, and tells her. The old woman stirs to life and starts walking.

The chariot drives into the camp, to the heavy clatter of Hector's armor, and pulls up. Andromache doesn't stir. Hecuba arrives. The women make way for her. She gasps.

HECUBA
Hector's armor ...

A soldier orders Andromache to get down. She obeys. The soldier is about to give a hand to Astyanax, but Andromache instinctively puts her arms around him and lifts him down herself. Hecuba moves toward the chariot.

HECUBA
Oh, sorrow, our sorrow ...

ANDROMACHE
Why should you weep?
This sorrow is mine.

HECUBA
O God—

ANDROMACHE
What has come to me is mine.

Hecuba throws herself at the chariot, reaching for Hector's shield, trying to touch it. Andromache springs to her side, the fierce antagonism of daughter and mother-in-law alive even in their grief.

HECUBA
Sons, noble sons, all lost.

ANDROMACHE

Oh, sorrow is here.

HECUBA

For me, for me.

ANDROMACHE

For the city in its shroud of smoke.

The soldiers pull the cart away. The two women stagger after it.

ANDROMACHE

Come to me, O my husband.

HECUBA

What you cry to lies in the grave.
My son, wretched woman, mine.

A soldier blocks their way.

ANDROMACHE

Defend me, me your wife.

HECUBA

My son, my eldest son,
whom I bore to Priam,
whom the Greeks used shamefully,
come to me, lead me to death.

ANDROMACHE
(Cries out wildly)
Death!

A long pause. The two women, suddenly still, look at each other united in their longing for death.

ANDROMACHE
(Quietly)
Oh, how deep a desire.

HECUBA

Such is our pain—

ANDROMACHE

For a city that has fallen, fallen.

HECUBA

For anguish heaped upon anguish.

ANDROMACHE
(Flaring again)
For the anger of God against Paris,
your son, who laid Troy's towers low,
to win an evil love.
Dead men—bodies—blood—
vultures hovering . . .

Astyanax runs up to his mother. Hecuba looks at her, spent,
unable to fight back. Andromache's eyes mellow with compassion as she chokes back her tears.

ANDROMACHE
(Gently)
Mother of him whose spear brought death
to Greeks unnumbered, you see what is here.
Driven like cattle captured in a raid—
My child and I—

HECUBA
(In a pitiful, almost childlike voice)
It is fearful to be helpless. Men just now
have taken Cassandra—forced her from me.

ANDROMACHE
And still more for you—more than that—

HECUBA
Number my sorrows, will you? measure them?
One comes—the next one rivals it.

ANDROMACHE
Polyxena lies dead upon Achilles' tomb,
a gift to a corpse, to a lifeless thing.

HECUBA
(Stunned, not quite assimilating the terrible news)
My sorrow.
That is what Talthybius meant—
I could not read his riddle. Oh, too plain.

ANDROMACHE
I saw her there
and covered her dead body with my cloak—

HECUBA

(Cries out)
Murdered—my child. Oh, wickedly!
Oh, cruelly slain.

ANDROMACHE

She has died her death, and happier by far
dying than alive.

HECUBA

Life cannot be what death is, child.
Death is empty—life has hope.

Moving Astyanax over to the women, leaving him in their care, Andromache tries to help the old queen with the only weapon she has, words—applying them like a hot iron to an open wound.

ANDROMACHE

Mother, O mother, hear a truer word.
I say to die is only not to be,
and rather death, than life with bitter grief.
She is dead, your daughter—to her the same
as if she never had been born.
She does not know the wickedness that killed her.
While I—I aimed my shaft at good repute.
I gained full measure—then missed happiness.
For all that is called virtuous in a woman
I strove for and I won in Hector's house,
knew well in what I should rule him,
and when give him obedience.
And this report of me came to the Greeks
for my destruction. When they captured me
Achilles' son would have me.
I shall be a slave to those who murdered—
O Hector my beloved—shall I thrust him aside,
open my heart to the man that comes to me
and be a traitor to the dead?
And yet to shrink in loathing from him
and make my masters hate me—
one night, men say, one night in a man's bed
will make a woman tame—

Her voice snaps as the sinister thoughts fluttering in her brain give way to the memory of the man she loved.

ANDROMACHE

O Hector, my beloved, you were all to me,
wise, noble, mighty, in wealth, in manhood, both.
No man had touched me when you took me,
took me from my father's home
and yoked a girl fast to you.
        (*The horrible reality breaking through again*)
And you are dead, and I with other plunder
am sent by sea to Greece. A slave's yoke there.
        (*Swinging round and facing Hecuba, wildly*)
Your dead Polyxena you weep for?
What does she know of pain like mine?
The living must have hope. Not I, not any more.

She has run out of words and stands there, erect, withdrawn
in her own hopelessness. The woman holding Astyanax edges
him forward slowly. Tentatively, the child approaches his
mother and touches her dress.

Hecuba is rooted to the spot—her eyes looking out as if across
time. She speaks in a flat, colorless voice that seems to come
from far.

HECUBA

Those ships—I have never set foot on one,
but I have heard of them, seen pictures of them.
I know that when a storm comes the
    sailors do their best.
But if great ocean's raging overwhelms them,
they yield to fate.
They give themselves up to the racing waves.
So in my many sorrows I am dumb.
I yield, I cannot speak.

She focuses on Andromache and her eyes stir back to life.
She approaches her slowly.

HECUBA

But, O dear child, let Hector be,
and let be what has come to him.
Your tears will never call him back.
Give honor to him who is your master.
Your sweet ways—use them to allure him.

Andromache steps back horrified, but Hecuba grips her arm.

HECUBA

So doing you will give cheer to your friends.
Perhaps this child, my own child's son,
You may rear to manhood and great aid for Troy.
And if you should have more children,
they might build her again.

The two women look at each other, held together by the
dawn of some impossible dream.

HECUBA

Troy once more be a city!
Oh—one thought leads another on.

The women around are also suspended in the dream. Camera
tracks across. One of them notices something which breaks
the spell. She shifts uneasily. The others do the same. Seeing
them, Hecuba too looks off and her face darkens. She steps
back apprehensively. Only Andromache remains still lost in
her thoughts.

Talthybius rides up and dismounts. He walks slowly forward.
He seems troubled, ill at ease. He stops at some distance from
Andromache. The women hold their breath.

TALTHYBIUS

Wife of the noblest man that was in Troy,
O wife of Hector, do not hate me.
Against my will I come to tell you.

Andromache looks at him. He goes on haltingly.

TALTHYBIUS

The people and the kings have all resolved—

ANDROMACHE

What is it? Evil follows words like those.

TALTHYBIUS

This child they order—

He can't finish the phrase—he looks away and mumbles
through clenched teeth.

TALTHYBIUS

Oh, how can I say it—

Andromache instinctively presses Astyanax close to her.

ANDROMACHE

Not that he does not go with me to the
same master—

TALTHYBIUS

No man in Greece shall ever be his master.

Pause. Andromache looks at him with perplexed, supplicating eyes.

ANDROMACHE
(In a small, tremulous voice)
But—leave him here—all that is left of Troy?

TALTHYBIUS

I don't know how to tell you. What is bad,
words can't make better—

ANDROMACHE
(Hoping against hope)
I feel you kind. But you have not good news.

Another silence. And brusquely, awkwardly, Talthybius
blurts it out.

TALTHYBIUS

Your child must die. There,
now you know the whole, bad as it is.

Andromache is frozen to the spot. Slowly, as if from the marrow of her bones, the scream comes—wild, scaringly, rising
from the dark roots of sound beyond words. Talthybius goes
on helplessly.

TALTHYBIUS

It was Odysseus had his way. He spoke
to all the Greeks.

ANDROMACHE

O God.

TALTHYBIUS

He said a hero's son must not grow up—

ANDROMACHE
(Turning on him)
God, on his own sons may that counsel fall.

TALTHYBIUS

—but from the towering wall of Troy be thrown.

Wildly, like a frenzied beast, Andromache presses her terrified son to her loins, covering him with her arms. As Talthybius approaches she backs away from him, swinging the child out of his reach, stumbling, moaning, infecting the women around with gathering frenzy.

Like some hunter stalking his prey Talthybius keeps circling around, shouting, desperately trying to get through to her, while the women flutter around like terrified birds.

TALTHYBIUS
Now, now—let it be done—that's wiser.
Don't cling so to him. Bear your pain
the way a brave woman suffers.
You have no strength—don't look for any help.
There's no help for you anywhere. Think—think.
The city gone—your husband too. And you,
a captive and alone—one woman—how
can you do battle with us? For your own good
I would not have you try—

He is almost upon her. She trips and falls yelling.

Hecuba and the women scream and rush at Talthybius, beyond themselves. He jumps back yelling furiously while the soldiers hold them back with their spears.

TALTHYBIUS
Hush—never a curse upon the Greeks.

Still on the ground, Andromache grips Astyanax in her arms, her force spent. Talthybius approaches and speaks to her in a low, compelling voice, as if trying to get through to her subconscious.

TALTHYBIUS
If you say words that make the army angry
the child will have no burial, and without pity.
So bear your fate as best you can.
Then you need not leave him dead without a grave.

A slight nod from Andromache. He helps her up gently.

TALTHYBIUS
And you will find the Greeks more kind.

Discreetly, controlling his emotion, he steps back and looks the other way, nodding to the soldiers to do the same.

One after another, the women turn their backs—creating a wall of privacy around Andromache's grief. She runs her hands over the child's shoulders and it is a long moment before she speaks. Camera tracks in.

ANDROMACHE
(Whispering)
Go die, my best beloved, my own, my treasure.

She slowly forces herself to look at him.

ANDROMACHE
Your father was too noble. That is why
they kill you. He could save others,
he could not save you for his nobleness.
(The pain bursting through)
My bed, my bridal—all for misery—
when long ago I came to Hector's halls
to bear my son—oh, not for Greeks to slay
but for a ruler over teeming Asia.
Weeping, my little one? There, there.
You cannot know what waits for you.
Why hold me with your hands so fast,
cling so fast to me?
(Laughing through her tears)
You little bird, flying to hide beneath my wings.
(A second outburst, wilder this time)
And Hector will not come—he will not come
up from his tomb, great spear in hand, to save you.

She freezes, her bruised brain trapped in an all-too-real nightmare.

ANDROMACHE
How will it be? Falling down—down—

With her eyes she traces the fall.

Flash. Camera tumbles down through space of shimmering whiteness.

As Andromache's eyes register the end of the fall, she swings her head away, gasping.

ANDROMACHE
Oh horrible.

She looks around again, with heartbreaking tenderness.

ANDROMACHE
And his neck—his breath—all broken.
And none to pity.

But he is still there, alive, warm, and she is invaded with the
physical need of him.

ANDROMACHE
You little thing,
curled in my arms, you dearest to your mother,
how sweet the fragrance of you.

She goes down on her knees, quickly, as if in a panic that she
may not have enough time.

ANDROMACHE
Kiss me—never again. Come, closer, closer.
Your mother who bore you—put your arms
around my neck.
Now kiss me, lips to lips.

The boy, confused, kisses her, then hugs her, remaining with
his arms tightly clasped around her neck. Her pain gradually
turns into wild fury and she finds release in hate.

ANDROMACHE
O Greeks, you have found ways to torture
that are not Greek.
A little child, all innocent of wrong—
you wish to kill him?
O Helen,
many the fathers you were born of,
Madness, Hatred, Red Death, whatever poison
the earth brings forth—God curse you
with those beautiful eyes that brought
    to shame and ruin
Troy's far-famed plains.

She flings the child away from her, yelling.

ANDROMACHE
Quick! Take him—seize him—cast him down.
Feast on his flesh—

The women turn round and scamper in panic. The little boy,
lost, terrified, runs up to his grandmother and clutches her
dress tightly.

The women hold Andromache, who is on the point of collapse.

ANDROMACHE

I cannot—
I cannot save my child from death.
Oh, hide my head for shame and fling me
into the ship.

A terrible silence. Hecuba can't bear to look at the child pathetically clinging to her.

HECUBA

Child, son of my son, whose toil was all in vain,
what can I do for you, poor piteous child?
Why wait? For what?

She gently pushes the boy away from her. He stands there looking around with plaintive, uncomprehending eyes. Talthybius moves toward him. Astyanax flies back to his mother and grips her tightly around the waist. She throws her head back, as if stabbed, her eyes closed, her mouth open in a silent scream. In the deadly silence, Talthybius walks up and puts a kind hand on the boy's shoulder, drawing him away.

TALTHYBIUS

Come, boy, let go.

The boy looks at him and, reassured by his kindness, obeys. Talthybius leads him up to the waiting soldiers.

TALTHYBIUS

Take him away.

Flanked by two soldiers holding spears, Astyanax starts to walk away. Talthybius can't bear to look. He mutters fiercely, almost an apology for the women to hear.

TALTHYBIUS

A herald who must bring such orders
should be a man who feels no pity,
and no shame either—not like me.

Astyanax and the two soldiers walk past the women frozen in their pity and hatred.

Talthybius waves to the chariot with Hector's armor to move up.

The hollow sound of the clattering metal stirs Andromache back to life. Slowly, like an automaton, she walks toward it. Talthybius helps her up. She turns and looks at the women with bland, unseeing eyes, drained by shock.

ANDROMACHE
(In a strange, matter-of-fact voice)
You know—
I have lost my child.

The women struggle to hold back their tears as the chariot moves off toward the ships, with Andromache standing motionless in front of Hector's shining armor. Only the rhythmic sound of drums can be heard from the Greek camp.

Astyanax, tiny between the soldiers, walking away.

Andromache on the cart, the sea in the background.

The women motionless, counting time, their hate building up in the blazing sun.

Outside Helen's hut, two armed guards lean on their spears, half dazed with exhaustion. Camera tracks in. We see Helen's eyes gliding along the wide cracks in the wooden walls, watching.

Helen's viewpoint: the women, tense, waiting. A soldier approaches Helen's hut with a jar of water. He fills the metal cups that the guards hold out, then a basin standing nearby. Some women walk up, looking at the water pleadingly. The guards wave them away. They don't move. One of the guards goes up and starts dispersing them.

Helen is looking at the other guard, who is unaware of her. She knocks softly. He turns.

HELEN
(More an order than a plea)
Water.

He looks the other way, unsure, suspicious. She knocks again, louder. Flustered, the guard approaches the basin and kicks it with his foot close to the open gap at the base of the hut. Quickly it is pulled out of sight.

Some of the women have seen. A roar of indignation goes up. They press toward the hut, shouting. Quickly they are joined

by more women. Their mood grows more dangerous by the
second. The soldiers vainly try to hold them back. They call
for help.

The women left in one of the enclosures stir dangerously.
They join in the shouting and press against the fence. Some
climb over. The soldiers knock them back violently. Someone
(Soldier 1) rides off to call for reinforcement.

Helen provocatively hangs her clothes over the top of the
wooden wall, evidently in order to wash herself. Through the
cracks, her naked body can be glimpsed briefly.

Like furies the women start flinging stones against the hut.
The soldiers have great difficulty in holding them back. The
sound of bugles is heard in the distance.

Outside the city walls. Astyanax and the two soldiers are
walking toward the walls. We hear the confused sounds from
the women's camp and, closer, the bugles alerting the Greeks.
Horses ride past.

Soldier 1 rides up and calls out to someone who comes galloping toward him. Several others gather round on horseback.

SOLDIER 1
(Shouting)
Find Menelaus.
Tell him to come quickly to the women's camp.

SOLDIER 2
What's up?

SOLDIER 1
They're after Helen's blood.

Soldier 2 rides off to alert Menelaus.

SOLDIER 3
I'd like to see them tear her limb to limb.

SOLDIER 1
You would, but I'm the one they'll hang for it.

SOLDIER 3
Why? They said they'd kill her.

Soldier 1 rides off waving to the others to follow him. Resent-
fully they do, camera following. The dialogue is continuous.

SOLDIER 4

No matter what they said,
Helen will get back home alive.

SOLDIER 5

And she knows it.

SOLDIER 4

They need her for the victory parade.
A symbol of Greek strength.

SOLDIER 5

A bloody trophy.

SOLDIER 3

Who needs her for a trophy? There's all that gold.

SOLDIER 4

(Ironically)

The Greeks don't go to war for gold.
They find a cause. That's what Helen is—a cause.

SOLDIER 5

Who wants a dead cause?

In the women's camp. Soldiers ride up and start dispersing
the rioting women.

The enclosure is surrounded and the last of the numbered
women are led off in a heavily guarded column. As they go,
Menelaus, followed by his personal guard, comes riding
toward the camp. His name passes among the women's lips.
They shout after him:

WOMEN

Kill her . . . Kill her . . .

Menelaus pulls up inside the camp and surveys the scene.
The soldiers are now in control and hold back the women
with joined spears. There is silence. Menelaus dismounts. He
looks at the women. The soldiers shout to them to kneel and
start forcing the ones who are closest to them, down. Defiantly the women kneel, turning their backs as they do, pay-
ing homage to Hecuba, who stands apart and remains standing. A soldier next to Menelaus is about to run up to her, but
Menelaus restrains him, realizing who she is.

With quiet, burning intensity, Hecuba speaks as if in prayer.

HECUBA

O thou who dost uphold the world,
thou past our seeking, hard to find,
God or Necessity of what must be,
or reason of our reason,
Whate'er thou art, I pray to thee—
seeing the silent road by which
All mortal things are led by thee to justice.

She walks slowly forward. The women rise behind her, silently reiterating her prayer. She stops at some distance from Menelaus. After a moment he speaks. It is clear that he is a vain man, unsure of himself, trying to project an image of strength—and trying too hard.

MENELAUS

Justice there will be.
The men who fought and toiled to win her back,
have given her to me to kill . . .
   (A short pause)
Or else, if it pleases me,
to take her back to Argos.

Helen's eyes through the cracks, watching. They register his words with a glint of satisfaction.

HECUBA

Kill her, Menelaus. You will?
Oh, blessings on you.

Menelaus turns to his guards and shouts ferociously.

MENELAUS

Seize her and drag her out by that long
blood-drenched hair.

The guards run off toward the hut.

HECUBA

But shun her, do not look at her.
Desire for her will seize you, conquer you.
For through men's eyes she gets them in her power.
She ruins them and ruins cities too.
Fire comes from her to burn homes,
magic for death. I know her—so do you,
and all these who have suffered.

But Menelaus is not listening. His fury has evaporated into

nervousness and insecurity at the thought of seeing her after
so many years.

The bodyguards burst into the hut.

The women watch tensely. The soldiers hold their spears in
readiness. Only Menelaus looks the other way—and Hecuba
looks at him.

After several moments, Helen appears. She has discarded her
cloak and wears a provocatively clinging dress. She is cool,
controlled, and beautifully groomed. Once out of the door,
she stops and takes in the scene. The bodyguards spring on
either side of her. One is about to grip her by the arm, but
she stops him with a quick, disdainful gesture. Relaxed, un-
hurried, she walks toward Menelaus, with the bodyguards
keeping their distance. She passes close to the women held
in check by the spear-holding soldiers. Their eyes spit hatred.

Disregarding them, steadily looking at Menelaus, Helen
stops near him. He avoids looking at her.

HELEN
(With injured dignity)
Menelaus, these things might well make a woman fear.
Your men with violence have driven me from my room,
have laid their hands upon me.

She moves into his line of vision.

HELEN
You haven't changed.

He swings away. She smiles.

HELEN
Of course I know—almost I know—you hate me,
but yet I ask you. What is your decision,
yours and the Greeks? Am I to live or not?

MENELAUS
(In a forced, harsh voice)
Nothing more clear. Unanimous in fact.
Not one who did not vote you should be given me,
whom you have wronged, to kill.

A sharp, savage roar goes up among the women.

Helen smiles.

HELEN

Am I allowed to speak against the charge?
To show you if I die that I shall die
most wronged and innocent?

MENELAUS

I have come to kill you, not to argue with you.

HECUBA

Oh, hear her. She must never die unheard.
Then, Menelaus, let me answer her.
The evil that she did in Troy you do not know.
But I will tell the story.
So she never can escape.

MENELAUS
(Resenting all this pressure, snapping)
That means delay.

But as he swings round at Hecuba, Helen steps in nimbly in
front of him. This time he doesn't turn away, for a long
moment.

MENELAUS

Still—if she wants to speak,
she can.
(Justifying his change of mood to Hecuba)
I grant her this because of what you say,
not for her sake. She can be sure of that.

HELEN
*(With the bitter resignation of innocence trapped in
the judge's prejudice)*
And perhaps, no matter if you think I speak
the truth or not, you will not talk to me,
since you believe I am your enemy.

A pause. Menelaus stands there in embarrassed and obstinate
silence.

HELEN

Still, I will try to answer what I think
you would say if you spoke your mind,
and my wrongs shall be heard as well as yours.
(Switching to the attack with brilliant effect)
First. Who began these evils?
(Pointing at Hecuba)

> She, the day when she gave birth
> to Paris. Who next was guilty?
> The old king who knew the stuff his son was made of
> and let him roam the world
> to ruin Troy and me.

She checks her gathering rage, not wanting to go too far too
soon.

HELEN

> I know what you are thinking.
> Why did I go—steal from your house in secret?
> That man Paris, or any name you like to call him,
> his mother's curse, oh, when he came to me,
> a mighty goddess walked beside him.
> Love, Aphrodite, tempting him with my beauty
> whispering promises that she would give me to him.
> And you, poor fool, what did you do?
> You threw your doors wide to the royal guest
> and spread your sails for Crete,
> left Sparta, left him in your house.

Before Menelaus can react to this hint of deserved cuckoldry,
she switches to a bit of soul-searching.

HELEN

> Ah well, not you but my own self I ask,
> what was there in my heart that I went with him,
> a strange man, and forgot my home and country?
> Not I—but Aphrodite.
> Punish her. Be mightier than the gods
> who rule the world but are her slaves.
> She is my absolution.
> So I went. Then see what happened!
> My abduction brought all Greece
> great good. No strangers rule you,
> no foreign spears, no tyrant.
>   (Exploding)
> Oh, it was well for Greece but not for me,
> sold for my beauty and reproached besides,
> when I deserved a crown.

Even the women are momentarily stunned by her glorious
insolence; then a rumble of indignation goes up. Hecuba
restrains them.

HECUBA

Let her finish.

Helen, satisfied, withdraws her claws and goes on with her own cross-examination.

HELEN

One thing with seeming justice you might say.
When Paris died in battle,
I should have left his house—gone to the Greeks.
Just what I tried to do—oh, many times.

Menelaus registers surprise and she goes on quickly.

HELEN

I have witnesses—the men who kept the gates,
the watchmen on the walls. Not once, but often
they found me swinging from a parapet,
a rope around this body, stealthily
feeling my way down.

Menelaus is taken in. She pauses, suspended in the memory of those cold, perilous nights.

HELEN

The Trojans no longer wanted me but Deiphobus,
the man who next took me—and by force—
would never let me go.

Feeling him ripe she moves in quickly for the kill.

HELEN

My husband, must I die, and at your hand?
Is that your justice?
I was forced—by violence.

She touches his arm. He doesn't pull away. Tremulously, she draws closer to him, until her whole body touches him, seeking refuge in his strength.

HELEN

I lived a life that had no joy, no triumph.
In bitterness I lived a slave.

He slowly turns and looks at her. Her beautiful eyes glisten with tears.

HELEN

I wish that like a painter I could have wiped out
my beauty from my face and had an uglier one.

He is riveted to the spot, helpless, mesmerized by her physical
proximity.

The women, horrified, tighten around Hecuba.

WOMAN 5

O Queen, defend your children and your country.

WOMAN 6

Her soft, persuasive words are deadly.

HECUBA

(Stepping forward)

Her gods will fight on my side while
I show her for the liar that she is.

That's what the women needed to revert to the attack. Like
birds of prey they sweep around Helen and Menelaus, shocking him back to reality. He shakes himself free and steps
away from her. Helen looks at the women furiously, who now
form a menacing wall around her.

HECUBA

Never make gods out fools to whitewash your own evil.
My son was beautiful exceedingly.
Your own desire was enough.
No need of any goddess. You saw him
in his Eastern dress, all bright with gold
and thought, once free from Sparta and in Troy,
where gold, you thought, flowed like a
    river, you would spend
and spend until your spendthrift hand
had drowned the town.
Your luxuries, your insolent excesses,
Menelaus' halls had grown too small for them.
And when you came to Troy and on your
    track the Greeks,
and death and agony in battle,
if they would tell you, "Greece has won today,"
you would praise this man here, Menelaus,
to vex my son. Then Troy had victories,
and Menelaus was nothing to you.

Looking to the successful side—oh yes,
you always followed there.
And now you talk of ropes—letting your body down
in secret from the wall. Who found you so?
Was there a noose around your neck?
A sharp knife in your hand? Such ways
as any honest woman would have found
who loved the husband she had lost?
Often and often I would tell you: Go,
my daughter. I will help you. I will send you
past the lines to the Greek ships.
Oh, end this war. But this was bitter to you.
In Paris' house you had your insolent way.
You liked to see the Eastern men fall at your feet.

Her indignation suddenly bursts into rage.

HECUBA

Look at that dress you wear, your ornaments.
Is that the way to meet your husband?
Oh, men should spit upon you.
Humbly, in rags; trembling and shivering;
so you should come, with shame at last,
instead of shamelessness,
for all the wickedness you did.

There is a terrible desperation behind her rage, an awareness
of the inadequacy of words and the futility of her hate. She
pulls herself together and goes on in a quiet, hollow voice.

HECUBA

King, one word more and I am done.
Give Greece a crown, be worthy of yourself.
Kill her.

Menelaus stands there flushed, at a loss for words.

WOMAN 5

O King, now show that your are worthy
of your fathers.

WOMAN 6

The Greeks called you a woman,
shamed you with that reproach.

WOMEN

Be strong, be noble. Punish her.

Irritated, resentful of the pressure, Menelaus snaps back hysterically.

MENELAUS

I see it all as you do. We agree.
She left my house because she wanted to,
went to a stranger's bed. Her talk of Aphrodite—
big words, no more.

He turns to Helen. Miraculously, beautiful tears are again streaming down her cheeks.

MENELAUS

Go. Death is near.
You shall not any more dishonor me.

He waves to his guards. Melodramatically, Helen throws herself at his feet.

HELEN

No! No! Upon my knees—see, I am praying to you.
It was the gods, not me.

HECUBA
(Springing to his side)
The men she murdered. Think of those
who fought beside you.

A WOMAN
(Yelling)
Of their children too.

HELEN

Oh, do not kill me. Forgive.

HECUBA

Never betray them. Hear that prayer.

MENELAUS
(Roughly, freeing himself from Helen's grasp)
Enough, old woman. She is nothing to me.

Helen lies limply on the ground, the very picture of wronged, defenseless femininity. The guards are now close, unsure of what they must do, perhaps hoping they will be ordered to kill her.

Suddenly, unexpectedly, she grabs a dagger hanging from a guard's belt and raises it as if to plunge it in her bosom. Like lightning, Menelaus seizes her hand and flings away the dagger. The women gasp. A flash of triumph goes through Helen's eyes.

MENELAUS
(Avoiding the women's eyes, righteously)
Her death in Troy is not the way.
I shall take her overseas,
with swift oars speeding on the ship,
and there in Greece, give her to those to kill
whose dearest died because of her.

He nods to the guards who lift Helen up.

MENELAUS
So in the end she will become a teacher,
teach women chastity—no easy thing,
but yet her utter ruin will strike terror
in their silly hearts.
(A beat)
Even women worse than she.

He walks to his horse and mounts it quickly.

HECUBA
(A last, desperate appeal)
Not with you! She must not set foot on your ship!

MENELAUS
And why? Her weight too heavy for it?

HECUBA
A lover once, a lover always.

Menelaus looks at Helen, who is pulling herself together.

MENELAUS
Not so, when what he loved has gone,
(To the guards)
Take her to the ships.

The guards grab Helen violently. She cries out.

MENELAUS
And keep her safe until she sails.

Disdainfully Helen shakes herself free and starts to walk away, provocatively forcing the guards to open a path for her among the women.

Menelaus spurs his horse and gallops away. In their frustration, the soldiers start pushing back the women.

As she goes, Helen turns back for a last look—then walks forward with an elated, assured step.

The women stumble back in confusion. Their faces, wild with indignation, fill the frame.

WOMAN 1
(Cries out)
Do you care, do you care,
do you heed these things,
O God, from your throne in high heaven?

WOMAN 2
Oh, if only far out to sea
the crashing thunder of God
would fall down—

WOMEN
Down—

WOMAN 2
—on Menelaus' ship . . .

WOMEN
Crashing *down* upon her oars.

WOMAN 12
And Helen too, with her mirrors of gold,
looking and wondering at herself
as pleased as a girl,
may she never come to the land of her fathers!

WOMAN 3
Never see her city!

WOMAN 2
The hearth of her home.

Helen rises into frame, as she steps nimbly on to the deck of Menelaus' ship. The wind is blowing. She shakes her head, letting her hair tumble down around her shoulders. She breathes deeply, then turns. Menelaus stands farther back, looking at her. Hold.

High on top of the city walls. Astyanax (in close up) struggles
to keep his balance in the strong, whistling wind. He looks up
at the soldier standing next to him. His eyes show that readiness to trust that is part of a child's fear. The soldier's rough
hand awkwardly touches the little head. The boy smiles. Now
the hand turns the head away, to no longer see the trusting,
luminous eyes. Gripped with fear, the child backs away from
the precipice, trying to cling to the soldier's legs. But the
hand is strong and the resistance offered to it supplies the
necessary impetus to finish quickly with the horrible, in-
escapable task.

Reeling, the camera plunges down through shimmering light
of blinding whiteness.

A ship's sail snaps open with a loud crack. Camera glides
down across its shuddering whiteness to a woman's face—
Andromache's—staring out toward the land. A man's hand
reaches into frame and touches her hair. She closes her eyes.

The sun is sinking behind the walls. The wind drives waves of
dust through the women's camp, adding to the sense of
desolation. Amid the now empty enclosures, the women stand
in silence, awaiting the signal of departure. The white dust
on their dresses and in their hair makes them seem like figures
hewn out of rock. Something makes them stir—something
coming their way. They exchange glances. One or two move
slightly forward, then they all turn and look at Hecuba, who
stands some way back. Sensing the approach of some new
and terrible trial, the old woman walks forward among the
women, her eyes scanning the dusty distance.

Talthybius and four soldiers dismount in the distance. Talthybius is holding in his arms the lifeless body of Astyanax.
He walks forward followed by a soldier who carries the large
bronze shield of Hector. Talthybius stops facing Hecuba and
the women. In the silence only the sound of the wind is heard.

TALTHYBIUS
One ship has sailed already, Hecuba,
and with it went Andromache,
the dead boy's mother.
In your arms, she told me, I must lay him
for you to cover the body, if you still
have anything, a cloak left—

He moves up to Hecuba, who slowly lifts her arms and receives the child.

TALTHYBIUS
(Choking back his emotion)
And this bronze-fronted shield that was Hector's,
she begged that he might lie upon it in his grave.

He backs away, trying to hide his confusion.

TALTHYBIUS
One trouble I saved you.
When we passed Scamander's stream
I let the water run on him and washed his wounds.

Hecuba says nothing, just looks ahead through him, past him.

TALTHYBIUS
I am off to dig his grave now.
Working together, you and I, will hurry to the goal.
When you have laid him out,
We'll heap the earth above him, then
up with the sails.

He turns to the soldiers and nods. The one carrying the shield comes forward.

HECUBA
Set the shield down.

The soldier does.

HECUBA
I wish I need not look at it.

Talthybius walks away quickly toward the other soldiers waiting in the distance.

Slowly, painfully, Hecuba brings herself to look at the child in her arms. And as if stabbed, she looks away again.

HECUBA
Beloved, what a death has come to you.
If you had fallen fighting for the city,
if you had known strong youth and love,
if we could think you had known happiness
—if there is happiness anywhere—

She stops, leaving the words suspended in their futility. She
kneels slowly and lays the child on the shield.

One after another, the women kneel behind her.

Bent over the shield, Hecuba moves her hands gently over
the bruised body without touching, as if afraid to hurt it.

HECUBA

Poor little one. How savagely our ancient walls
have torn away the curls your mother's fingers wound
and where she pressed her kisses—here
where the broken bone grins white . . .

She snaps.

HECUBA

Oh no—I cannot—

But there is no escape from the terrible reality and now she
focuses on the boy's hands. She folds them with infinite
tenderness.

HECUBA

Dear hands, the same shape your father's had,
And dear proud lips forever closed.
False words you spoke to me,
when you would jump into my bed
and tell me, "Grandmother, when you are dead,
I'll cut a lock of hair and ride with all my soldiers
past your tomb."
Not you, but I, old, homeless, childless,
must lay you in your grave, so young,
so miserably dead.
What could a poet carve upon your tomb?
"A child lies here whom the Greeks feared and slew."
Ah, Greece should boast of that,
the fear that comes when reason goes away.

She turns slightly and speaks to the women.

HECUBA

Come, bring such wreaths for the pitiful dead body
as you can find. God has not left us much
to make a show with.

Two women rise and go toward an old, solitary olive tree.

HECUBA

Anything I have I give you, child.

She slowly unwinds the long shawl draped over her head.
Her short-cropped gray hair gleams in the twilight.

Two of Talthybius' soldiers are seen coming back.

HECUBA

O men, secure once good fortune comes—
fools, fools.

The women approach with olive branches and kneel on either
side of her. Hecuba raises the shawl over the shield. The
women sway and start singing a lament. The funeral rite has
begun. Ceremoniously, Hecuba shrouds the dead body, her
voice rising in incantation.

HECUBA

Oh, not because you conquered when the horses raced,
or with the bow outdid your comrades,
your father's mother lays these wreaths beside you
and of all that was yours, gives you
this covering.

WOMAN

(Lamenting)
Oh, this was once our prince, great in the city.

HECUBA

So on your wedding day I would have dressed you,
the highest princess of the East your bride.

She lays the wreaths over the shrouded body.

The soldiers approach. They nod that the time has come for
the burial.

Four women walk over and stand on either side of the shield.
Hecuba nods and they raise it slowly, she and the rest of
the women stand up.

HECUBA

I heal your wounds. With linen I bind them.
Ah, in words only, not in truth—
a poor physician.
But soon among the dead, your father
will care for you.

Slowly the cortege falls in behind the soldiers and moves toward the grave.

A soldier stands near the grave holding a torch. Talthybius stands back respectfully as the procession approaches and stops. The walls of the city loom in the thickening darkness. The women don't stir, postponing the last terrible moment. But obeying a silent order from Talthybius, the two soldiers jump into the grave, ready to receive the shield. The women look at Hecuba.

WOMAN 1

You, O child, our bitter sorrow
earth will now receive.

WOMEN

Mourn, oh mother.

HECUBA

Mourn indeed.

WOMAN 2

Weeping for all the dead . . .

WOMEN AND HECUBA

Weeping, weeping . . .

WOMAN 1

Your sorrows that can never be forgotten.

HECUBA

Go: lay our dead in his poor grave.

The women with the shield carry it over to the grave. Hecuba turns away.

HECUBA

I think those that are gone care little
how they are buried. It is we, the living,
our vanity.

The soldiers take the shield and start lowering it into the grave. And all at once the pent-up emotion bursts.

WOMEN

(They cry out)
Beat, beat your head.

HECUBA
(*Topping them*)
Vain, vain the bulls we slew . . .
our nightlong prayers . . .

The shield has disappeared into the ground.

The women gather round Hecuba.

HECUBA
And yet—had God not bowed us down,
not laid us low in dust,
none would remember us or tell our wrongs
in stories men will listen to forever.

Camera pulls back slowly, holding the group of women
silhouetted against the walls. A melee of sounds builds up—
horses, men shouting, wheels running on stony ground.
Camera swings round to show several horses galloping toward
the walls. Their riders hold large torches.

Soldiers with torches are climbing up and some are already
at the top. A voice booms out.

VOICE
Captains, attention. You have been given charge
to burn this city. Do not let your torches sleep.
Hurry the fire on.

The soldiers start flinging their torches into the city.

In the flickering light of the flames which gradually build up,
the women huddled around Hecuba stumble away from the
walls in confusion.

The horses rear, ready to bolt. Talthybius jumps on his.

TALTHYBIUS
(*Shouting over the noise*)
You women—
whenever a loud trumpet call is sounded
go to the Greek ships to embark.
(*To Hecuba*)
Old woman, I am sorriest for you.
(*Waving to the soldiers*)
Follow.

He rides ahead.

Slowly, painfully, the women move forward, accompanied by Talthybius' soldiers.

Flames are now leaping above the walls as more and more buildings are heard crashing to the ground.

Camera tracks with Hecuba and the women. A strange, crazed look comes into the old woman's eyes as she accelerates her step, moving along the walls toward a gate, through which pours a fiery glow.

HECUBA
(Mumbling)
Hurry, old feet . . . a little nearer . . .
there, where I can see my city,
say good-bye to her . . .

The women struggle on after her, their terror rising.

Hecuba is getting nearer and nearer to the gate.

Seeing her, Talthybius turns his horse round, yelling.

TALTHYBIUS
Stop them!

The soldiers block the women's way and head them off.

Hecuba stumbles back in horror as she looks through the gate at the raging flames.

HECUBA
O, God!

She looks around her wildly.

HECUBA
What makes me say that word?
The gods I prayed, they never listened.

She breaks into a run toward the gate. Against the blinding blaze, we see Talthybius jump off his horse, spring up to her and grab her. Their bodies dance grotesquely, liquidlike, as they struggle. Talthybius lifts her up and staggers away.

Talthybius, with Hecuba in his arms, joins the rest of the women.

TALTHYBIUS
Out of her head, poor thing, with all she's suffered.

He puts Hecuba down and lets her fall into the arms of the
women, who form a tight circle around her.

TALTHYBIUS
Hold her. Don't be too gentle.

And he runs off to find his horse.

Tight frame of women's heads looking up, around Hecuba's
which leans limply, face down, on the women's shoulders.

WOMAN
O Lord, father who made us,
you see your children's sufferings?

WOMEN
Have we deserved them?

The glow flares up with sudden tremendous intensity.

WOMAN 2
Look!

The fire lights the whole town up.

WOMAN 12
The citadel—it is all flame now.

WOMAN 1
Troy is vanishing.
What was left is rushing up in smoke.

WOMEN
First the spear and then the fire.

The circle shudders and breaks as the soldiers start pushing
them forward. As they stumble on in confusion, Hecuba looks
back toward the burning city.

HECUBA
Children, hear, your mother is calling.

WOMEN
  (Yelling)
They are dead, those you are speaking to.

HECUBA
My knees are stiff, but I must kneel.
  (Kneeling)
Now, strike the ground with both my hands.

One after another the women kneel. Vainly the soldiers try
to stop them.

WOMAN 12

I too . . .

WOMAN 2

I kneel upon the ground . . .

WOMAN 1

I call to mine down there.

WOMAN 3

Husband, poor husband . . .

They begin to strike the ground with their hands as they
invoke the dead.

HECUBA

They are driving us like cattle—taking
us away.

WOMEN

Pain, all pain.

HECUBA

Priam, Priam you are dead,
and not a friend to bury you.
The evil that has found me—
do you know?

WOMAN 3

No. Death has darkened his eyes.

WOMEN

He was good and the wicked killed him.

WOMAN 1

Fall and be forgotten. Earth is kind.

They fall flat on the ground. Furiously the soldiers start to
pull them up. The women struggle.

WOMAN 4

The dust is rising, spreading like a
great wing of smoke.

WOMAN 13

I cannot see my house.

WOMAN 2

The name has vanished from the land,
and we are gone, one here, one there,
and Troy is gone forever.

A great deafening crash is heard, making the earth shake.

HECUBA

Did you hear? Did you know?

WOMEN

(A *huge cry*)
The fall of Troy.

The women moan and sway as the thunder subsides.

WOMAN 1

Earthquake and flood and the city's end.

No one moves. Even the soldiers are overawed by the moment. In the silence, a trumpet sounds. Hecuba looks up. With proud deliberate strength she rises to her feet, a figure of timeless endurance.

HECUBA

Trembling body—old, weak limbs,
you must carry me on to the new day of slavery.

Drawing from her strength, one after another the women rise. With a steady step Hecuba walks through them and away toward the ships. The women fall in behind her.

In the glow of the burning city, they walk away into the night, getting smaller and smaller . . .